‹NORWAY›

MAJOR WORLD NATIONS

NORWAY

Ralph Zickgraf

CHELSEA HOUSE PUBLISHERS
Philadelphia

Chelsea House Publishers

Contributing Author: David Klein

Copyright © 1999 by Chelsea House Publishers,
a division of Main Line Book Co.

3 5 7 9 8 6 4 2

Library of Congress Cataloging-in-Publication Data

Zickgraf, Ralph.
Norway / Ralph Zickgraf.
p.   cm. — (Major world nations)
Originally published: New York : Chelsea House Publishers, 1989,
in series: Places and peoples of the world.
Includes index.
Summary: Surveys the history, geography, economy, government,
people, and culture of Norway.
ISBN 0–7910–4747–4
1. Norway—Juvenile literature.   [1. Norway.]
I. Title.   II. Series.
DL409.Z5   1997
948.1—dc21   97–17788
CIP
AC

◄ C O N T E N T S ►

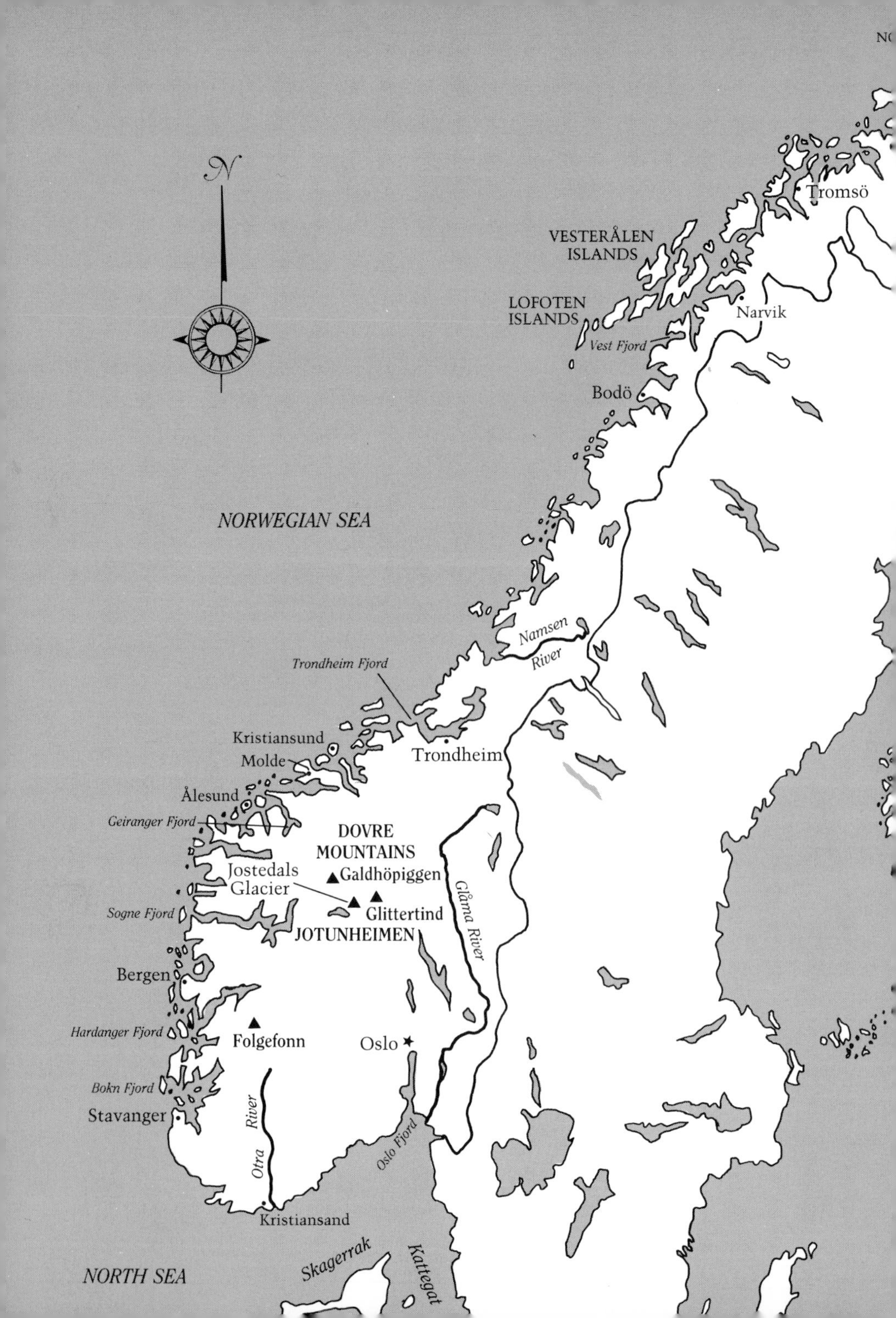

N

Tromsö

VESTERÅLEN
ISLANDS

LOFOTEN
ISLANDS

Narvik

Vest Fjord

Bodö

NORWEGIAN SEA

*Namsen
River*

Trondheim Fjord

Kristiansund
Molde

Trondheim

Ålesund

Geiranger Fjord

DOVRE
MOUNTAINS

▲Galdhöpiggen

Jostedals
Glacier

Glåma River

▲
Glittertind

Sogne Fjord

JOTUNHEIMEN

Bergen

Hardanger Fjord

▲Folgefonn

Oslo ✦

Bokn Fjord

Stavanger

*Otra
River*

Oslo Fjord

Kristiansand

NORTH SEA

Skagerrak

Kattegat

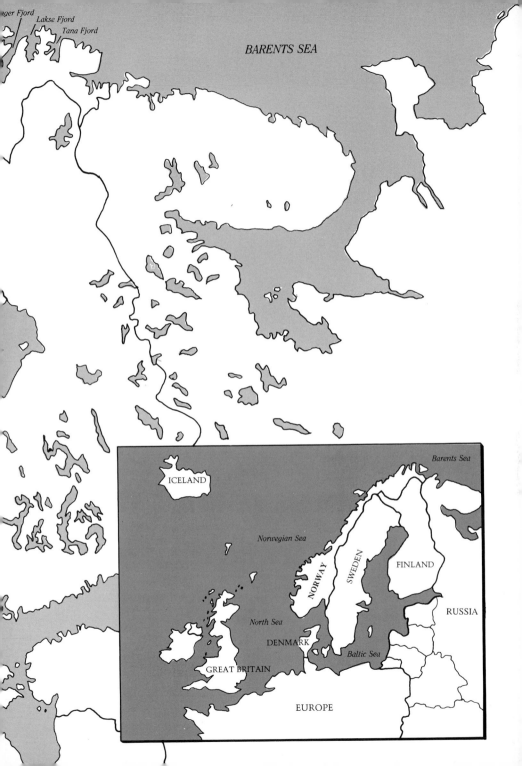

ager Fjord
Lakse Fjord
Tana Fjord

BARENTS SEA

ICELAND

Norwegian Sea

Barents Sea

NORWAY

SWEDEN

FINLAND

RUSSIA

North Sea

DENMARK

Baltic Sea

GREAT BRITAIN

EUROPE

◄ FACTS AT A GLANCE ►

Land and People

Official Name	Kingdom of Norway (Kongeriket Norge)
Location	On the west side of the Scandinavian Peninsula; bordered on the east by Sweden and in the northeast, above the Arctic Circle, by Finland and Russia
Area	125,182 square miles (324,221 square kilometers)
Highest Point	Glittertinden 8,104 feet (2,470 meters)
Climate	Temperate (south) arctic (north)
Population	4,383,807
Population Density	34 persons per square mile (13 per square kilometer); lowest in Europe
Population Distribution	75 percent urban; 25 percent rural
Capital	Oslo (population 483,401)
Major Cities	Bergen (population 221,717), Trondheim (population 142,927), Stavanger (population 103,496)
Official Languages	Bokmål and Nynorsk
Other Languages	Samí (Lapp) in the north; most Norwegians also speak English
Official Religion	Church of Norway (Evangelical Lutheran)

Ethnic Groups	Almost all the population is of Norwegian descent; there are some 20,000 Samí (Lapps). A small but growing minority consists of industrial workers from Africa and Asia who have taken up permanent residence

Economy

Major Products	Oil and natural gas, machinery, ships, fish, paper and other wood products, iron, steel, and aluminum
Major Resources	Oil and natural gas deposits in the North Sea, water power for hydroelectric energy, ferrotitanium ore, and forests
Employment of Labor Force	Services, 71 percent; industry, 23 percent; agriculture, forestry, and fishing, 6 percent
Currency	*Krone* (plural *kroner*), divided into 100 *ore*

Government

Form of Government	Constitutional monarchy
Formal Head of State	King
Head of Government	Prime minister
Eligibility to Vote	All citizens age 18 and older
Legislature	Unicameral parliament, called the Storting

◄HISTORY AT A GLANCE►

around 11,000 B.C.	Stone Age hunter-gatherers enter Norway.
2000–1500 B.C.	The Germanic ancestors of today's Norwegians invade Norway.
330 B.C.	The Greek trader Pytheas visits Norway; Norway is first mentioned in classical writing.
A.D. 100	The Iron Age begins in Norway.
800–1100	During the Viking Age, Norwegian Vikings raid Iceland, Scotland, and the Hebrides Islands.
870	Norwegian Vikings colonize Iceland. Harald Hårfager (Fairhair) becomes Harald I, first king of Norway.
911	The Norwegian Viking Rollo invades France and settles in Normandy.
around 985	Erik the Red colonizes Greenland.
around 1000	Leif Eriksson sails to North America.
around 1020–50	Norway is converted to Christianity.
1050	King Harald Hardraade (Hard Ruler) founds Oslo.
1130–1300	Civil wars weaken the country, and the Hanseatic League gains control of much of Norway.
1339–50	The Black Death strikes Norway; one-third of the population dies.
1380	Norway is united with Denmark.

1397	The Union of Kalmar unites Norway, Denmark, and Sweden.
1536	Norway becomes a province of Denmark. Lutheranism is declared the state religion.
1814	Denmark gives Norway to Sweden in the Treaty of Kiel but keeps Norway's colonies. Norway declares independence and adopts a constitution. After brief hostilities, Sweden takes possession of Norway but promises to observe the constitution.
1854	Norway's first railroad is completed.
1884	The cabinet of Norway becomes responsible to the parliament instead of the king.
1885	Electricity is used for the first time in a Norwegian factory.
1905	Norway dissolves the union with Sweden and becomes independent.
1911	Roald Amundsen reaches the South Pole.
1914–18	Neutral Norway loses half its merchant fleet to German action during World War I.
1935	The Labor and Farmer's parties form a reform government that begins the establishment of a social-welfare system.
1940–45	German troops invade and occupy Norway in World War II.
1949	Norway joins the North Atlantic Treaty Organization (NATO).
1957	King Haakon VII dies and is succeeded by Olaf V.
1991	King Olav V dies and is succeeded by his son, Harald V.
1994	Norway voters reject participation in the European Union.

‹ NORWAY ›

Norway's fjords are world famous. These deep, narrow inlets of the sea are surrounded by steep mountains and line the coast of Norway from north to south.

Norway and the World

On the very rim of Europe, ice-capped mountains loom over stormy northern seas. Here, in a land of rock, snow, lakes, rivers, and precious little soil, a race of tall, fair, blue-eyed people have created a nation.

Norway is a mountain plateau sliced by deep canyons that bring the ocean far into the land. At its widest, Norway is only 200 miles (320 kilometers) across, and fully three-fourths of its people live within sight of the sea. Not surprisingly, since early times they have been fishermen and sea rovers. Their ancestors, the Vikings, ranged all over the North Atlantic and discovered Iceland, Greenland, and the coast of North America long before other Europeans. In later years the Norwegians pioneered whaling in Antarctica, deep-sea fishing, and international trade in all the oceans of the world. They also built many of the ships for these tasks. At the beginning of the 20th century, Norwegian shipyards led the world in the total carrying capacity of ships produced.

Today, Norway reaps another harvest from the sea. Together with Great Britain, it explored, mapped, and developed the North Sea oil fields. This involved drilling and pumping oil from giant

Drilling platforms house pumps to bring oil from deep beneath the frigid Barents and North seas to fuel Norway's economy.

floating platforms in some of the world's roughest waters. Although the oil shortage of the 1970s gave way to the oil glut of the 1980s, both Norway and Russia are looking to exploit the rich oil deposits under the northern Barents Sea. There, the ordinary problems of deep-sea drilling will be complicated by the extreme cold, but Norwegian ingenuity will no doubt find a way.

Life in Norway has always been a struggle with the elements—with snow and rain, with cold and arctic darkness. The growing season is short and most of the fields are steep and stony, so farmers also had to be fishermen, trappers, and loggers in order to survive. These conditions have bred self-reliant, hardy people who love nature. In the past, Norway's resources have not always been enough to support all of its people, and Norwegians struck out to build new lives in other lands. One thousand years ago, they journeyed to Ireland, Greenland, France, and as far south as Constantinople (now Istanbul) in Turkey. In the late 19th century, a wave of Norwegian immigrants helped to settle and tame the northern plains of North America.

In the 20th century, however, Norway has become one of the world's most industrialized nations, with one of the highest standards of living in the world. Many of the country's rushing streams and roaring waterfalls now run through turbines and generators in giant hydroelectric plants. They are Norway's "white gold"—an abundant source of cheap and clean energy to power factories, plants, and railroads and to heat and light homes and offices.

Norwegians are proud people with a great love of their country. For centuries they were dominated by Denmark and Sweden, and they managed to achieve full statehood only after a long struggle. In 1905, Norway declared independence from Sweden and, crowning a Danish prince as king, became a constitutional monarchy.

In 1940, "little Norway" gave the Nazi war machine its first real test by resisting German invasion for two months. Even after German bombs forced the king and government to flee, most Norwegians, fired by a fierce love of liberty, resisted the German occupation in every way possible throughout the war.

Over the centuries, Scandinavia was isolated from the rest of Europe by distance and climate. It was off the main road of migration, invasion, sometimes even of trade. This isolation had both advantages and disadvantages for Norway. The Norwegians maintained a strong ethnic and cultural identity. They were spared some of the wars and upheavals that mainland Europe suffered—but when changes came, they reached Norway late. For instance, the Industrial Revolution came to Norway a full century after it came to England.

Today, Norwegians realize Scandinavia is no longer set apart from the rest of Europe or the world. The experience of invasion and occupation in World War II has taught Norway that no nation can "go it alone." Norway is a charter member of the United Nations and full member in the North Atlantic Treaty Organization (NATO). Norwegians staff UN peacekeeping units stationed in trouble spots around the world, and the Norwegian army, navy, and air force participate in all NATO military operations. In addition, Norway takes part in many aid programs around the world. Through the Norwegian Agency for International Development and the Asian Development Bank, it sends money, teachers, and medical aid to such nations as Tanzania, Kenya, India, and Bangladesh.

Despite the nation's important trade relations with members of the European Union (EU), Norwegian voters in 1994 decided not to join that organization. The country has been, however, a member of the European Free Trade Association (EFTA). In addition, through an agreement of the Nordic countries, citizens of Finland, Sweden, Norway, Denmark, and Iceland have the freedom to work and live anywhere in Scandinavia.

There are many contradictions in Norway today. The tough, self-reliant, conservative Norwegians are members of a lifelong social-welfare system more complete than that of many socialist countries. Norwegians revere their king, yet they have a passion for equality, scoff at titles, and insist that there are no social classes in their country.

Busy fish markets demonstrate the country's continuing reliance on the ocean, sometimes called Norway's "blue meadow."

Norwegians are outdoorspeople who increasingly find themselves working indoors. Many Norwegians think of themselves as simple farmers and fisherfolk, but each year more and more of them move to the cities. Their jobs are far from simple, too—they are computer programmers, medical technicians, engineers, and designers.

Almost every Norwegian belongs to the Evangelical Lutheran Church of Norway, yet the majority of people go to church only for weddings. If a Norwegian worships anything, it is nature. But in the rush to industrialize and urbanize, and in spite of extraordinary care, Norway's air, land, and water have suffered greatly from pollution.

To meet the challenges, threats, and confusions of the world today, Norway still has its best resource—Norwegians. They are the vigorous and confident inheritors of a proud history, which they are determined to carry well into the future.

For thousands of years, sailors on the way northward—from Viking explorers to modern vacationers—have been greeted by the spectacular sight of Norway's coastline.

The Way
Northward

From the far northeastern corner of Europe, above the Arctic Circle, a mountainous peninsula extends south for some 1,000 miles (1,600 kilometers). To the east it is bounded by the Baltic Sea. Its rugged western and northern coasts are washed by the Norwegian Sea and the Arctic Ocean. The southern end of this enormous rocky finger is separated from mainland Europe by two narrow arms of the North Sea, the Skagerrak and the Kattegat. This is the Scandinavian Peninsula, and along the western and northern side of its central north-south mountain range is the rugged and beautiful land of Norway.

The eastern side of the peninsula is Sweden. East of Sweden across the Gulf of Bothnia (the northern arm of the Baltic Sea) is Finland. A smaller peninsula that juts northward from mainland Europe is Denmark. Some 645 miles (1,032 kilometers) to the west is the island nation of Iceland, discovered and colonized by the ancestors of today's Norwegians. Together, these five nations make up Scandinavia, set off from the rest of Europe and linked to each other by geography, climate, history, and culture.

Norway is a long country, wide at the top and bottom and thin in the middle. At its thinnest, just above the Arctic Circle, it is only

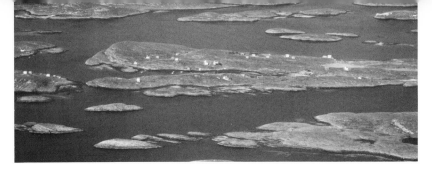

Hundreds of sparsely settled, rocky islets called skerries spread through the sea off the coast of Norway. This range is just beyond the city of Bodö.

about 40 miles (64 kilometers) wide between the Norwegian Sea and Sweden. The land border that it shares with Sweden, Finland, and Russia is 1,569 miles (2,510 kilometers) long. Norway's coastline is even longer — 1,643 miles (2,628 kilometers). However, if the coastline were straightened out, it would stretch for more than 12,000 miles (19,200 kilometers). This is because Norway is pierced by many long inlets of the sea, called fjords.

Along the coast are some 50,000 islands and skerries, or rocky islets. The fjords and the island-fringed coast are ice free year-round because of the Gulf Stream. (The Gulf Stream is a current of warm water in the North Atlantic that flows from the Gulf of Mexico northeast along the coast of North America to Nantucket, then east to the North Sea. One of its branches, the North Atlantic Current, splits, and one portion runs north along the shores of Norway.) As long as people have lived in the steep valleys and on the rocky shores of Norway, they have traveled by this protected coastal seaway rather than struggle over the endless mountains or on the open sea. The very name of the country reflects the importance of this ancient highway: In Norse, the language the Scandinavians once shared, Norway means "the way northward."

Geology

Norway presents a forbidding face to those who approach it along this watery highway. Waves break against dark walls of rock that rise in sheer cliffs. Above the cliffs are steep, forested slopes topped by bare granite or snowcapped peaks. Almost three-fourths of the country's 125,182 square miles (324,221 square kilometers) consists of mountains.

These mountains are made up of bedrock dating from the formation of the earth's outer layer, or crust. In the billions of years since then, the bedrock was covered by oceans that laid down thick layers of sedimentary rock. The bedrock and the sedimentary layers were then twisted, folded, and thrust high above sea level by the movements of the solid outer layers of the earth. Long periods of intense cold (ice ages) caused huge glaciers to creep across most of the Northern Hemisphere. As the glaciers advanced, these ponderous rivers of ice scraped the mountaintops of Norway down to the bedrock and gouged deep canyons between them. The weight of the immense ice fields pressed down the mountains, so much so that much of what is now Scandinavia was again under sea level. When the climate warmed and the glaciers melted, they left deposits of their debris—boulders, gravel, and silt—in valleys on the mountains' flanks. Freed of the weight of ice, the land rose above the sea again. But the sea still filled the deep, narrow canyons that snake far into the interior—Norway's distinctive fjords. And the glacial deposits in the high valleys became pockets of soil, which generations of sturdy farmers cleared of stones and boulders to produce highland fields and meadows.

Above the fields and meadows, lakes fill glacier-carved hollows. There are more than 160,000 lakes in Norway. Many of the high peaks are topped year-round with snow and ice. Streams trickle and tumble down the mountainsides, growing into fierce rivers, white with rapids. Lacy waterfalls spill from tree-covered cliffs to silent, brimming fjords. Sod-roofed barns, pagoda-shaped churches of vertical log construction (called stave churches), and brightly painted wooden houses dot the mountainsides and glimmer from the wooded banks of the fjords. Nature and humans have combined to produce a landscape that is astonishingly varied and beautiful.

Climate

Although Norway lies as far north as Alaska and Siberia, its climate is much less arctic than the climates of those regions because of the Gulf Stream. This river of warm water from the tropics keeps the coast and fjords free from ice; it also produces currents of warm, moist air that flow over Norway's coastal regions. The annual mean temperature of Bergen, on the west coast, is 45° F (7° C); that is 54° F (12° C) higher than average for that latitude. Farther north, in the Lofoten Islands above the Arctic Circle, the annual mean temperature is 77° F (25° C) higher than the global average for so far north. Winters along the coast are mild, and summers are cool and wet. Bergen reminds many visiting Londoners of their rainy native land; it receives 80 inches (203 centimeters) of precipitation, mostly rain, per year.

When the moist southerly winds created by the Gulf Stream hit the mountains on Norway's coast, the air rises and gets colder. The change in temperature causes the air to drop its load of moisture in the form of rain, sleet, or snow. After crossing the mountains, the air is drier, and, as a result, so is the interior of Norway. Meteorologists (weather scientists) say that the interior is in the rain shadow of the mountains. The average annual precipitation in eastern Norway is less than half that in the Bergen area.

Summers are warmer inland, with more sunny days than on the coast, but winters are colder. Winter temperatures in the interior often go below -22° F (-30° C). In Finnmark, a county in the far north, temperatures as low as -60° F (-51° C) are not uncommon.

On the coast and in the interior, winters are long and dark, and summers are brief and bright, as in all arctic countries. In the winter, the sun rises late and sets early; in Hammerfest, the world's northernmost city, it does not appear at all from the middle of November until the middle of January. Even in Oslo, about 800 miles (1,280 kilometers) to the south, winter days are so short that streetlights

Rondane National Park, located east of the Jotunheimen, is noted for its unusual mountain formations.

stay on until 10:00 or 11:00 A.M. and must be turned back on by 2:00 or 3:00 P.M.

In the summer, however, the sun climbs high in the sky. In northern Norway—called the Land of the Midnight Sun—the sun does not set at all from the middle of May to the end of June. In the southern part of the country, daylight lasts until 10:00 or 11:00 P.M., and the twilight lasts until the small hours of the morning.

These extremes of light and dark have a great influence on many aspects of life in Norway, from agriculture to psychology. Not every plant can thrive in the fleeting northern summer, and the long winter night can cast gloom on all but the most resilient spirit.

Plants and Animals

More than 2,000 species of plants grow in Norway, in spite of the short growing season. Spruce and pine forests grow in inland valleys; the floors of the forests are covered with leafy mosses and heather. Deciduous trees (trees that shed their leaves in the fall) grow in all regions except the far north. These trees—birch, aspen, rowan, and ash—cover the steepest hillsides and flourish higher in the mountains, where the air and soil are too thin for spruce and pine. This area, called the birch zone, begins at about 2,800 feet (952 meters) and extends to about 3,900 feet (1,330 meters) above sea level. Above the birch zone is the willow belt. Here, dwarf willow and dwarf birch trees, twisted by the wind into grotesque shapes, cling to the stony ground in dense knee-high mats.

In the south and north are treeless mountain plateaus called *vidda*. In the late summer, these huge plains are vividly colored with the red, gold, and purple of heather and bilberry bushes. Blueberries, blackberries, and cranberries are also common throughout the country. Even the cloudberry finds a home in Norway. This yellow berry is the fruit of a member of the rose family that grows only in Scandinavia and a few places in the British Isles.

Norway, like other arctic countries, has many fur-bearing inhabitants, ranging in size from small, mouselike lemmings to polar bears. Lemmings have long attracted the world's notice because, once or twice every 20 years or so, thousands of them join in year-long mass migrations from one part of Norway to another. Polar bears do not live in mainland Norway, but they roam the Norwegian islands of Svalbard, high in the Arctic Ocean. A small herd of musk oxen lives in a nature reserve on an island off the northwest coast.

Martens and sables (two fur-bearing mammals related to weasels), wolverines, bears, and lynxes were once common throughout the country. Until about 100 years ago, trade in these animals' skins

Polar bears live on the islands of Svalbard, a Norwegian possession far to the north of the Arctic Circle.

This modern Samí, one of the few who still follow the reindeer across the tundra, sports the traditional four-pointed, down-insulated cap. He sits in front of a hut made from reindeer hides.

was an important part of the economy. Today, the larger animals of prey can be found only in the more remote mountains. But martens and several kinds of foxes still roam the lowland forests of the south as well as the vidda of the north. Beavers make their lodges in lakes all over Norway, and badgers can be found in many a woodland thicket.

A few wild reindeer still live in the mountain areas in the south. In the north, large herds of half-tame reindeer can be found, tended by the Samí (Lapp) herders, who have followed the herds' migrations over the north of Europe for thousands of years. Elk live in the inland spruce and pine forests, and red deer thrive in the cold, wet hills of the west coast, just as they do in the similar climate of northern Scotland.

Fish of many kinds have always been important inhabitants of Norway. Seafood is a major part of the Norwegian diet, and fishing is an important part of the Norwegian economy. Fish that live most of their life in the cold North Sea swarm into the warmer coastal waters to spawn (reproduce). Teeming schools of cod, haddock, and herring are close enough to the mainland for small fishing boats to reach. This kind of fishing has always helped Norway's farmers along the coast add to their larders and incomes—that is why they call the sea that surrounds them their "blue meadow."

Mackerel, sardines, and capelin (a small fish that, netted in the millions, is ground up into animal food and fertilizer) abound in the deeper offshore waters. Fleets of large trawlers sail from western and northern waters to harvest them.

Several species of whales pass through the Norwegian Sea on their annual migration to summer feeding grounds in the Arctic Ocean. Norwegians have long hunted these sea-dwelling mammals. A 4,000-year-old cave drawing on the island of Rödöy shows a man harpooning what looks like a small whale. The earliest written records, from the Middle Ages, show that men from Norway were part of the worldwide whaling industry. (Whales were killed primarily for their blubber, which produced valuable whale oil, used as a source of light and heat.) Norwegians were prominent in the development of the Antarctic blue whale fisheries in the beginning of the 20th century.

Modern whaling techniques, pioneered in large part by Norwegians, have been so efficient that the existence of many species of whales is threatened. Widespread public concern, roused by conservation groups such as Greenpeace, has led most whaling nations to agree to a moratorium, or agreement not to kill these animals.

Norway, along with Japan and Russia, has not completely agreed to the ban. Norwegians are reluctant to stop hunting whales for several reasons. Although the whaling industry is no longer vital to Norway's overall economy, it is important to certain small coastal communities. Just as important, perhaps, is the widespread feeling that whaling is an essential part of Norway's history and culture, and Norwegians treasure their culture. They are also stubborn and independent people, and they will never agree to anything merely because of world public opinion.

Norway has, however, put some restrictions on the whaling industry. In 1904, Norway declared its entire north coast a whale sanctuary—the world's first moratorium. And Norway strictly controls the numbers and kinds of whales killed and the way in which they are killed. Norwegian whaling is limited to smaller coastal species, such as the minke whale. Nevertheless, the International Whaling Commission continues to criticize Norway's policies.

Freshwater fish native to Norway's many lakes and rivers include perch, pike, and trout. Norway's cold, fast-flowing rivers are also famous around the world as the spawning ground of the Norwegian salmon.

Most kinds of fish can live only in fresh water or only in salt water. Salmon, however, are born in fresh water, then migrate downstream and into the ocean, where they spend their adult lives. They grow quite large (15 pounds, or 6.8 kilograms) on their diet of smaller fish. After two to five years (depending on the subspecies) each salmon returns to the river from which it came and fights its way upstream to the exact place of its birth, to spawn and die as the cycle begins again. No one has yet discovered how a salmon unerringly returns, over thousands of miles and after several years, to the same stretch of water where it hatched.

In addition to fish and whales, an amazing variety of birds come to Norway in the summer. During the long days of intense sunlight, millions of microscopic plants and animals thrive in the waters of the Arctic Ocean and Norwegian Sea. These tiny creatures, called plankton or krill, drift near the surface in dense clouds. Schools of tiny fish and huge baleen whales alike feed on these nutrient-rich clouds, called blooms. Larger fish come to feed on the smaller fish, and birds in the millions come every year to feed on the fish, to nest, and to hatch their young. The birds swarm on the cliffs and rocky islands of Norway's coastline. The Lofoten Islands in particular are home to huge colonies of seabirds—puffins, guillemots, cormorants, kittiwakes, and gulls. The rare sea eagle can be seen diving into the sea to snatch its dinner from the waves.

Ducks and geese of almost every species also pass by; Norway is on one of the world's greatest flyways for migratory birds. The northern cliffs are also the summer home of the eider. This sea duck lines its nest with down (fine feathers) to keep its chicks warm, and daring Norwegians scale the cliffs to rob the nests of down for their light and cozy eiderdown blankets.

Regions

There are many Norways. One is a modern industrial nation, with one of the highest standards of living in the world. That Norway is best seen in teeming metropolitan Oslo, where 900,000 people, roughly 20 percent of the population, live and work. But Norway is also a land of vast distances and solitude — at 34 persons per square mile (13 per square kilometer), the country has the lowest population density in Europe.

To most people, even many Norwegians, Norway is a land of fishermen and farmers. Today, however, only about 6 percent of the labor force is employed in fishing, agriculture, and forestry combined. In fact, only 3 percent of all the land in Norway is even arable (capable of being cultivated).

Norway is Norwegians, people who for the most part share a common Nordic ancestry. Almost three-fourths of the population have pure blue eyes and blond hair. Yet their customs and dialects vary widely from region to region. They like to say that if a Norwegian knows eight languages, seven of them are Norwegian.

The majestic Jotunheimen range, the "Home of Giants," is also home to the largest ice field in Europe.

Norway's mountains are the reason for the many different Norways. They divide the country into four traditional regions: the northern, central, western, and eastern areas. Each is different in climate, soil, and heritage, and each, until the 20th century, was cut off from the others except by sea. Before the age of the automobile and the plane, it took less time for someone to travel from Bergen to Scotland than to reach Oslo, Norway's capital, from Bergen.

The border with Sweden runs along the top of the north-south mountain range called Kjölen ("the Keel," because it reminded the seafaring Norse of the keel of an overturned boat). In Norway's bulbous southern half, a north-south chain of ranges called Langfjellene (the Long Mountains) divides Ostlandet (eastern Norway) from Vestlandet (western Norway).

The highest and wildest range in the Long Mountains is Jotunheimen (Home of Giants). This range contains Scandinavia's tallest mountains — Glittertinden at 8,104 feet (2,470 meters) and Galdhöpiggen, only slightly shorter. The Home of Giants is also the site of Jostedalsbreen (-*breen* means "glacier"), Europe's largest ice field, which covers 300 square miles (780 square kilometers).

North of Jotunheimen, the east-west Dovre range separates eastern Norway from central Norway, also called Tröndelag (the Trondheim region). Central Norway includes the Trondheim lowlands, which are wide (for Norway), flat areas with rich soil. Beyond Tröndelag is the fourth region, Nord-Norge, or northern Norway. Cut off from the rest of the country by a narrow neck of mountains, by distance, and by its arctic climate, northern Norway includes one-third of the land area of Norway and has less than 12 percent of the population.

In northern Norway, the long, cold winters provide plenty of opportunities for nearly everyone to enjoy outdoor sports, such as skating, sledding, and cross-country and downhill skiing.

Northern Norway

Running north for some 300 miles above the Tröndelag, the county of Nordland is merely the narrow western flank of Kjölen, less than 40 miles (65 kilometers) wide at spots. It is very steep and rugged country, deeply cut by many fjords. Although the last 40 years have seen roads and airports spread throughout Norway, many people and most cargo in this region still travel along the protected coastal waterway by coastal steamer or car ferry.

The Arctic Circle, the imaginary ring around the globe that marks the beginning of the earth's northern frigid zone, cuts across Norway near Mo i Rana. This old mining town, which before World War II had less than 1,500 inhabitants, is now the site of a huge state-owned steelworks. The largest such enterprise so far north, the plant produces more than 400,000 tons (406,400 metric tons) of steel per year. More than 15,000 Norwegians make their homes in a ring of tall apartment blocks around the old town. Nearby is Svartisen, Norway's second largest glacier, and Glom Fjord. This is a short, deep fjord below a mountain lake fed by glacial runoff. It is renowned for its wild beauty even in this land of beautiful fjords.

The first major stop above the Arctic Circle is Bodö, on Salt Fjord. Capital of Nordland, fishing port, and military outpost, Bodö

North of the Arctic Circle, Salt Fjord stretches past the city of Bodö, center of the Nordland province.

was almost completely destroyed by German bombs in 1940. The rebuilt town is brightly colored, clean, and very modern looking against its mountain backdrop. South of the town, where the fjord narrows between beetling cliffs, is the Saltstraumen maelstrom, a huge whirlpool created by each incoming or outgoing tide.

North of Bodö is the wide mouth of Vest Fjord (West Fjord). Offshore are the Lofoten Islands and, north of them, the Vesterålen Islands. The Vesterålens are low and flat, but the Lofotens are a row of rocky heights that thrust upward from the sea in a closely packed row that Norwegians call the Lofoten Wall. Svolvaer is the largest of the many fishing villages that cling to the Lofotens' rocky coasts. In February and March, the small harbors of these villages are crammed with fishing boats of every size and description. This is the cod season, and Norwegians come from far and near to net these ocean-dwelling fish as they swarm into the shallow coastal waters to spawn. Special excursion boats bring tourists out to watch the spectacle.

Things are just as hectic ashore, as the tons of fish are unloaded and processed. In large, modern plants, workers fillet the cod and package the frozen fillets for shipment around the world. The roe (fish eggs) is extracted and canned. Even the livers are canned for a Norwegian favorite, cod's liver stew.

Equally busy are the many small, independent fishing outfits. Many of these are farmers who have come to supplement their income by harvesting the blue meadow. They split the fish and spread them on wooden racks to dry in the sun, producing the traditional *törr-fisk*, a year-round staple of the Norwegian diet.

At the point where the Lofoten Wall comes closest to Norway, Ofoten Fjord knifes deeply into the mainland. Near the head of the fjord, only about 20 miles (32 kilometers) from the Swedish border, is Narvik. This wealthy little town is the shipping point for the giant iron mines at Kiruna in Sweden. The electric-powered trains of the Lofoten railway carry the ore over the mountains to this bustling port deep in the northern forest. Great ore ships wait in the middle of the fjord for their turn at the quays, where trains unload the ore into the freighters 24 hours a day.

Outside Narvik, there is little industrial activity in northern Norway. In the inland valleys and on the narrow strips of level ground along the fjords, people practice subsistence farming. Grain does not thrive so far north, but farmers can grow enough potatoes and vegetables and produce enough dairy products and meat to feed themselves and earn cash for other necessities. These hardy, self-sufficient folk also add to their incomes by logging, trapping, and fishing.

Houses, roads, and fish-processing plants pack the village of Svolvaer on one of the rocky Lofoten Islands off Norway's northwestern coast.

This rugged life, tied to the land and to the seasons, gives the Nordlanders their distinct character, self-confident but quiet and reserved. The long, dark winters and rough terrain sometimes mean isolation for them, but the precarious nature of life in the north has taught them to work together and depend on each other. They sometimes practice a sort of homegrown socialism—for instance, in worker-owned canning factories. Entire villages cooperate to start up, manage, and staff these enterprises.

Tromsö, capital of Troms, the county north of Nordland, is a center for fishing and canning. Narrow streets, horse-drawn carts, and log and wooden buildings along the waterfront hark back to Tromsö's frontier days, when whaling and sealing expeditions set sail from its wharfs. Tromsö is thoroughly modern, however, with supermarkets, an airport, a television station, and a cable railway. The longest suspension bridge in northern Europe connects the city, which is on an island, with the mainland.

Tromsö is also the site of the Observatory for Northern Lights. Here scientists spend the arctic nights studying the mysterious phenomenon called aurora borealis, or northern lights. These are bands of glowing colors that sometimes stream across the northern skies, forming shimmering arches or flowing curtains. The exact cause of these beautiful displays is still unknown, although scientists now believe they are connected with the concentration of electromagnetic solar energy at the earth's poles.

Hammerfest, the world's northernmost city, is also on an island. Like the rest of Finnmark, Norway's northernmost, largest, and least-populated county, Hammerfest was completely destroyed by the retreating German army in World War II. Lying at the foot of a steep, snowy mountain, this unlucky northern outpost has also been buried by avalanches and swept by fire several times. Hammerfest always rises again, chiefly because its ice-free harbor makes it an important center for shipping and trade with Finland and Russia.

For centuries Norwegian farmers have flocked to fishing stations such as Gamvik to harvest cod.

In 1891, Hammerfest became the first town in the world to install electric street lighting—not a luxury when you consider that the nights sometimes last eight weeks. Near the harbor is the Meridian Stone, a memorial to the first exact measurement of the earth, the achievement of an international scientific effort that lasted from 1819 to 1852.

It is only about 60 miles (96 kilometers) from Hammerfest to the North Cape, the northern tip of the continent. Mageröy (Meager Island) is a large, barren island separated from the mainland by a narrow channel. Its headland is North Cape, a sheer cliff of black granite rising over a thousand feet from the Arctic Ocean. The wide windows of a large hall at the top offer panoramic views of the top of the world. The North Cape Hall is ideal for watching the midnight sun roll along the horizon, passing without interruption from setting to rising.

The capital of Finnmark is Vardö, 120 miles (192 kilometers) to the east, on the shore of the Barents Sea. The coastline between North Cape and Vardö is rocky and barren, deeply cut by three immense north-south fjords—Porsanger, Lakse, and Tana. There are no farms, only scattered fishing villages. The roads are rough, and for much of the year mail and supplies are delivered by snowmobile.

South of Vardö, quite close to the border with Russia, is the tiny port and mining town of Kirkenes. This open-pit mine and its processing plant, where iron ore is separated and concentrated in pellets by a magnetic separating process, produce more than 1 million tons (1.02 million metric tons) of high-quality ore per year. The countryside is remarkably green, particularly compared to the desolate coast to the west. There are gentle hills that in the summer delight the eye with the very unarctic green of grass and birch leaves.

Finnmark draws anglers from around the world; many of the rivers that run down from the inland mountain plateau teem with trout and arctic char. Two of the best salmon rivers in the world are the Alta, west of Hammerfest, and the Tana, a long river that for much of its length is the border between Norway and Finland. Near the headwaters of the Tana, on the Finnmarkvidda, is the Sami village of Karasjök.

The Samí

Thousands of years ago, when the Nordic ancestors of the Norwegians and Swedes first came to Scandinavia, the Samí (or Lapps, as the newcomers called them) were already there. They were nomads, following their herds of reindeer in seasonal migration. They spent the winters on the vidda, then moved onto the northern tundra of Sweden or Norway in the summer.

Tundra is treeless arctic plain with permafrost—subsoil that remains frozen year-round. In summer the melted snow, instead of percolating through the permafrost, saturates the topsoil, producing a mucky black soil. The tundra in summer is lush with tough grass and dwarf herbs and shrubs that are excellent fodder for the reindeer. When the extreme arctic cold returns to the tundra, the Samí and their herds move back onto the vidda, where the winters are milder. The reindeer use their antlers to scrape away the snow and graze on the moss and heather below. Reindeer are the wealth of the nomadic Samí, who drink reindeer milk and eat huge quantities of reindeer

An 1896 photograph captures the Samí performing age-old tasks. Approximately 2,000 Samí still depend on their herds of reindeer for food and clothing, as did their ancestors.

meat and wild berries. They trade meat for necessities such as wool and salt and for luxuries such as sugar and tobacco. Much of their clothing and their wigwamlike shelters are made of reindeer hide.

The Samí are short and slender, and they have darker complexions than most Norwegians. Their traditional dress is distinctive: reindeer-skin boots and leggings and a *kofte* (tunic) of blue wool. In winter the "reindeer Samí" wear heavy fur coats and tall four-pointed caps stuffed with eiderdown. They are a peaceful people with a strong sense of community. Those who still tend the half-tame reindeer follow their herds across the north of Europe in complete disregard of national borders; the governments of Norway, Sweden, and Finland allow them to move at will across their frontiers. The Samí administer their hereditary grazing rights and settle most other such matters among themselves. They speak their own language, which is taught in the schools, where they send their children for 18 weeks of the year.

Most of the Samí, however, are no longer nomadic, or even seminomadic. Of the 20,000 Samí living in Norway today, only about 2,000 still follow the reindeer—and they use snowmobiles and live in houses during the winter.

As the Scandinavian countries continue to settle and modernize their northern territories, there is less wilderness for reindeer to roam. Modern life brings necessities and luxuries—snowmobiles, medical care, television—that the reindeer economy cannot supply. So most of the Samí now live on small farms or in remote villages. Besides farming, they work in mines, on construction and lumbering crews, and increasingly in factories and offices. They are determined, however, to keep their racial and cultural identity, along with their language.

Norway's Territories

Some 500 miles (800 kilometers) north of North Cape, an archipelago (a chain) of frozen islands stretches to within 650 miles (1,040 kilometers) of the North Pole.

Most of the islands' 24,000 square miles (62,400 square kilometers) are covered by glaciers. These islands are so far north that the winter night lasts for four months and the northern lights stretch into their southern sky. Together, they make up the Norwegian dependency of Svalbard. (A dependency is a territory that is under the legal or military jurisdiction of a nation but is not formally part of it.)

Dutch explorer Willem Barents discovered the islands of Svalbard in 1596, but until Norway claimed control of them in 1925, no one was very interested. From the 16th century to the 18th century no one visited the islands except sealers, whalers, and walrus hunters. In the late 19th century polar explorers used them as a jumping-off point for their dashes to the North Pole.

Norway's claim to the island group was made official in 1920 by the Treaty of Svalbard, which eventually was signed by 41 nations. The treaty gives all 41 nations the right to exploit the islands' minerals. Other than Norway, however, only Russia has risked the costs and dangers of mining and shipping so far north.

The prospect of Barents Sea oil tantalizes many people, but the obstacles are great. In addition to storms, drifting pack ice will threaten drilling platforms. There is also the question of ownership. Although the mineral exploitation rights in the Treaty of Svalbard include the seabed for four miles around each island, Norway claims the waters around these areas because they are over the Norwegian continental shelf. Russia also claims a big hunk of the Barents Sea, and the two claims overlap each other considerably. When the technology necessary to exploit the oil arrives, the dispute over these icy waters is sure to heat up.

The Russians also have strategic, or military, interests in Svalbard. The islands lie at the extreme northern reach of the Norwegian Current (an extension of the Gulf Stream). Russian submarines based at Murmansk need the ice-free waterway between Svalbard and Nor-

The Dutch navigator Willem Barents (after whom the Barents Sea is named) sought a northeastern passage to Asia in the 1590s. Instead, he discovered Spitsbergen and Barents islands, which became Norwegian territories in the 20th century.

way to reach the Atlantic. The Treaty of Svalbard bans all military installations, but the Russians maintain an airport there. Altogether, about 2,000 Russians live in Svalbard, compared to about 1,000 Norwegians.

Destroyed by the Germans during World War II, the coal mines of Svalbard have been reopened and now produce about 900,000 tons (914,400 metric tons) of coal each year. The skies are often dark, even during the summer, from the coal dust that spews from processing plants. To protect as much of the environment as possible from pollution, Norway has dedicated more than 40 percent of the land area of Svalbard to national parks and wildlife preserves. Wild reindeer and musk oxen roam the tundra, and polar bears stop by as they follow seals over the ice.

Norway has three other offshore possessions. Jan Mayen is an island in the Greenland Sea, approximately 300 miles (500 kilometers) east of Greenland. The island is presently 35 miles (56 kilometers) long and 9 miles (14 kilometers) across at its widest point. That could change, however, because it is actually the peak of an undersea volcanic ridge. Beerenberg, the volcanic mountain on the island's northern end, last erupted in 1732. The rest of the island is low, hilly tundra, home to a few arctic foxes.

Henry Hudson first sighted the island in 1607, and in 1614 a Dutch sea captain named Jan May claimed it for Holland. Whalers used it as a base until the whales were exterminated in the area, around 1642. The first humans to spend any time on the island were a team of Austrian weather observers who wintered there during the First International Polar Year (1882–83). In 1921, Norway built a weather observatory and radio station. On May 8, 1929, Norway claimed Jan Mayen as part of its territory. During World War II, the United States maintained a weather station on the island, and in 1958, NATO built an airstrip and radio navigation station. No one lives on Jan Mayen except the workers at the station.

In 1911, a Norwegian, Roald Amundsen, became the first person to reach the South Pole. Norway followed this triumph with extensive exploration of the southern polar regions. In 1930, a combined sea-air expedition discovered and explored a huge land mass in the Antarctic Ocean south of Africa. Rocky mountains, more than 11,000 feet (3,353 meters) high, rose from a vast, ice-covered plain. This vast plateau, six times the size of Norway, proved to be part of the continent of Antarctica. The explorers named the region Queen Maud Land, for the queen of Norway. In a royal decree signed in 1939, her husband, King Haakon VII, claimed Queen Maud Land for Norway. Then, in 1949, Norway formally declared Queen Maud Land a dependency.

A 1950 expedition of Norwegian, Swedish, and British scientists determined by seismic soundings that the ice sheet covering most of the region is as much as 1.5 miles (2.4 kilometers) thick. Nothing grows there, and no animals live there; penguins, seals, and seabirds visit it. There are no permanent human settlements, of course. Several countries have operated research stations on the coast.

In 1928, Norway added Bouvet Island to its holdings, and Peter I Island followed in 1931. These are two rocky islets in the Antarctic Ocean. Bouvet is about 1,000 miles (1,610 kilometers) north of Antarctica and 1,600 miles (2,600 kilometers) southwest of the Cape of Good Hope in South Africa. It was discovered by French explorer Jean-Baptiste Bouvet de Lozier in 1728. Rocky, with ice cliffs, it is extremely difficult to land on. Twenty-two square miles (57 square kilometers) in area, it rises from stormy seas to a height of 3,068 feet (935 meters). Peter I, an even smaller islet, was discovered by Russian explorers in 1821 and named for Czar Peter I, father of the Russian navy.

Just inland from Bergen in southwestern Norway, the village of Stalheim lies nestled amid steep mountains near the Flåm River.

Central and Western Norway

The lowland valleys of the Tröndelag region between the coastal mountains and Kjölen contain some of the most productive farmland in Norway. Farmers grow barley and potatoes and raise dairy cattle in the flat, fertile fields along the Namsen and Nid rivers. There is good farmland, too, along the wide Trondheim Fjord, which stretches far inland. Summers are rather cool and wet, but winters are mild, and the region is so productive that in some years the Tronders sell their excess hay to the British Isles.

When snow covers the fields, farmers head for the mountain logging camps. Thirty percent of the twin counties of Nord and Sör (North and South) Tröndelag is covered with pine and spruce forests. There are several mining villages in the mountains, too. The iron and copper mines of the region are not as productive as they once were, and mining in such difficult terrain is not always profitable. However, the mines provide important jobs, so the government keeps them open by subsidizing them, either by helping to pay their operating costs or by purchasing their ore at high prices. The copper-mining town of Röros, near the headwaters of the Glåma River, was founded in the 17th century, and most of the buildings from that time have since been carefully preserved. The played-out mines there closed in 1978 but have since been reopened as part of a unique open-air museum.

Trondheim

Trondheim is the center of the region and is the country's third largest city (142,927 inhabitants). It is an ancient city, founded in the 10th century by King Olaf I Tryggvason. During the Middle Ages, when it was called Nidaros, Trondheim was the capital of Norway.

Built on a peninsula between the Nid River and Trondheim Fjord and laced by canals, the city is a sort of watery, wooden Venice. Rows of warehouses, each painted a different color, stand on stilts along the riverside. The fjord waterfront teems with fishing boats, pleasure craft, coastal steamers, and stately white cruise ships (Trondheim is the starting point for the popular cruises to the Land of the Midnight Sun). The waterfront also has boatyards, several canneries, and a modern plant for deep-freezing fish. Just offshore is the little island of Munkholmen, with the ruins of a medieval monastery.

After it was devastated by fire in the 17th century, Trondheim was rebuilt according to a revolutionary town planning scheme that replaced most of its twisting streets and narrow alleys with broad, straight avenues. In the center of the city is a bustling marketplace, filled with vegetable, fruit, and fish stalls and overlooked by a giant statue of St. Olaf (Olaf II Haraldsson). Nearby is the Stiftsgarden, northern residence of the royal family, a vast wooden palace built in the ornate, heavily decorated style known as baroque.

On a hill across the river, the stone Kristiansten Fortress frowns over the landward approach to the city; in the days of the medieval kings it was an important defensive outpost. Also on the outskirts is the Folk Museum, where ancient homes, barns, and other buildings have been restored and stocked with authentic implements to re-create daily life in Trondheim during the Middle Ages.

Northeast across the fjord is Frosta, where the Vikings invented representative democracy. It is the ancient site of the *ting*, their council. The Viking chiefs met there annually to vote on matters of common concern, such as the election of a king. Every year from 940 until the 16th century, Norwegians sent their representatives to Frosta to pass laws and administer justice.

The Trondheim region is rich in history but still quite up-to-date. The outskirts of the city are studded with modern apartment blocks, each with its own parklike grounds and cluster of shops. The region is the center of the fast-growing Norwegian telecommunication and computerized service industries. Trondheim University's engineering and architectural graduates leave school to create buildings, bridges, and factories all over Norway and the world.

Like all Norwegians, the people of Trondheim are addicted to the outdoor life. In winter they flock to the ski center of Bymarka, 20 minutes by bus or train from the center of town. There are miles of groomed, lighted trails for cross-country skiing, a ski lift for Alpine skiers, and a popular ski jump.

Trondheim is also the gateway to year-round sport in the Dovre Mountains to the south. Hiking, mountain climbing, bird-watching, elk hunting, and fishing for trout and salmon are some of the ways Norwegians and European visitors entertain themselves in the summer and fall. In winter, of course, the major attraction is the skiing.

The Dovre railway takes eager skiers to Oppdal, which has the longest lifts and the most exciting ski runs north of Switzerland. To the west are more ski resorts in the Romsdal Alps, a jumble of mountains and wild valleys that run down to western Norway's northernmost fjords. The area has some of the world's highest waterfalls, such as the Mardalsfoss. Here water crashes from the cliff top in an uninterrupted fall of about 1,000 feet, then falls again for over 700 feet. In the spring, when the melting snow swells mountain streams, the Mardalsfoss becomes one breathtaking fall of well over 2,000 feet.

South of Oppdal is the Dovrefjell, a barren mountain plateau that rises in the south to Jotunheimen, the roof of Norway. Here the snow stays year-round, and so do the skiers; the ski lifts and trails on Galdhöpiggen and Glittertind are open through the summer.

From Jotunheimen the land falls away to the southeast in long valleys, such as Gudbrandsdal, Valdres, and Hallingsdal, whose rivers run into Oslo Fjord or the Skaggerak. To the west and southwest, the land drops much more steeply, and mountain waters rush more fiercely into the fjords of western Norway.

Norway's tumbling waters produce more than scenic waterfalls. Tunnels and turbines transform their energy to electricity. Besides powering hydroelectric plants, the water cools aluminum processing plants tucked into the mountain valleys. At Ardals Lake above Sogne Fjord, high-country water drops 3,000 feet (over 900 meters) to a generating station built inside a mountain, safe from bombs and avalanches. At Sunndalsora, at the head of a fjord near Kristiansund, water from the Dovre Mountains cools and powers a huge aluminum plant that produces more than 50,000 tons (55,800 metric tons) of aluminum a year.

The fishing town of Kristiansund stands on several islands connected to each other and the mainland by bridges and ferries. The town was completely rebuilt after being destroyed in World War II. Many earlier traditions persist, however. For instance, Kristiansund's dried cod is known as *klipp-fisk* (cliff-fish) instead of törr-fisk, because it is spread to dry on the rocks of the cliffs instead of on wooden racks.

Farther south along the west coast is Ålesund, the largest town (population approximately 36,000) in the northern part of western Norway. Spread like Kristiansund over a string of islands, Ålesund is Norway's herring capital. Next to cod, herring is the Norwegians' favorite fish.

Fishing is a chancy trade, however. Dangerous winter storms lash the coast—many a fishing boat has been lost. That is why so many of the skerries offshore have names such as Devils, Hard Skull, and Man Killer. Today, most boats are equipped with radio and other electronic equipment that helps them avoid being wrecked. A worse threat to the herring fleet is the disappearance of the herring. In recent years fewer and fewer schools have swum in from the ocean deeps to spawn in the shallow coastal waters. The people of Ålesund have responded to the decline in the herring catch by developing other industries, such as engineering and the manufacture of textiles and furniture. On Romsdal Fjord between Kristiansund and Ålesund, the elegant little town of Molde relies on tourism to support itself. Molde's many attractions include a beautiful waterfall in the middle of town and a panoramic view of 87 snow-covered peaks in the Romsdal Alps. This resort town offers sea and snow, sailing and skiing, mountain climbing and jazz festivals. In summer, the long days of sunlight and the cool, moist air produce so many blooming flowers that Molde can rightly call itself the City of Roses.

Warehouses, wharves, and factories crowd the shores of Ålesund, the center of the Norwegian herring- and seal-hunting fleets.

The Great Fjords

From Ålesund to Stavanger, the sea penetrates western Norway in a thousand places. There are tiny, twisting *viks* (creeks) and giant arms such as Sogne Fjord. Norwegians boast that even here, where the country is widest, practically no one lives beyond the smell of salt water.

Each fjord is different. Inland from Ålesund, Geiranger Fjord snakes between mountains that rise, sometimes straight from the water's edge, more than 6,000 feet (1,800 meters). At times the channel seems hardly wide enough for a boat to pass. High above the fjord, sod-covered barns are remnants of farms where the children playing by the farmhouse wore tethers to prevent them from slipping to their death. What look like handkerchief-size patches of green from below are upland fields so steep that resourceful farmers had to cultivate them by cable. With a winch stationed at the top of the slope, the farmer would use a sturdy Norse pony or, more recently, a gasoline engine to pull the plow straight uphill on a wire.

Geiranger Fjord still gets plenty of activity, however. Norwegians and foreign visitors alike flock here each summer, to hike, climb the rocks, or sail. Cruise liners visit year-round. Geiranger is the site of one of the most beautiful and famous waterfalls in Norway, the Seven Sisters. A mountain brook tumbles from the forested slope in 7 streams of silver that fall in a lacy cascade to the fjord 1,500 feet (460 meters) below.

Sogne Fjord is Norway's longest fjord (120 miles, or 192 kilometers). Like most fjords, it is quite deep in places—at one spot the bottom of Sogne Fjord is 3,700 feet (1,130 meters) below the waterline. The strip of land between water and rock is broader and greener than in Geiranger, and farming is still a major source of livelihood here. The fields are marked by miles of well-kept walls—millions of handpicked stones—that testify to generations of backbreaking labor. On the north shore, apple orchards take advantage of the south-

Built in the 12th century, Heddal Stave Church in Telemark is the largest of 33 stave churches that still stand in Norway. In the Middle Ages there were between 900 and 1,200 of these uniquely Norwegian structures, which combine Norse and Christian symbols in their decoration.

ern exposure. Even tobacco grows here, probably farther north than anywhere else in the world.

Sogne Fjord is a major waterway. Freighters bring bauxite, an ore, to the smelting plants at Ardal and Höyanger and carry aluminum away. Höyanger, which sits on a small arm of Sogne Fjord halfway along its northern shore, is a good example of Norwegian environmental planning. A tunnel carries smoke and fumes from the plant to the top of a nearby mountain, where, after being filtered and "scrubbed," it is released aloft.

Several stave churches still stand in remote villages along Sogne Fjord. The one at Borgund is a well-preserved example of this uniquely styled religious structure. Erected in the middle of the 12th century, when Christianity was still new to the Norse, it is constructed of huge, square-hewn logs. The roof and sides are covered with long shingles with rounded points. In addition to crosses, the builders decorated the church with carved wooden dragons, symbols from the old Norse religion. A worn, round hole in one wall enabled lepers, who were not allowed to enter, to listen to the priest.

Farther south, wide Hardanger Fjord slashes deep into western Norway on a northeastern slant. In the middle of the channel is the island of Varaldsöy, the rocky summit of a drowned mountain. On sunny days the white dome of Folgefonn, a 1,600-foot (500-meter) peak topped with snow all year, shines above cherry and apple orchards.

The southern arm of Hardanger, Sör Fjord, is celebrated in Norwegian music, literature, and painting. Composer Edvard Grieg was inspired by its beautiful mix of wild nature and lush rural peace. In the spring, the long stretch of orchards along the eastern shore is a stunning explosion of fluttering white and pink blossoms. At the southern end of Sör Fjord is Odda, an industrial center whose factories are carefully designed and managed to prevent them from destroying the region's charm.

Many of the thriving farms of the Hardanger district are quite old. The region is stable and conservative. Hardanger folk cling to the old ways. For instance, they still treasure their traditional costumes, which are compulsory wear for festivals, weddings, and other celebrations. The women wear long black dresses with tight white bodices. Over the dresses go long black aprons and short red jackets. The aprons and skirts are elaborately embroidered and sometimes beaded in bright colors. Girls braid their hair in matching ribbons, but married women wear white headdresses of starched linen. The men wear knee breeches and short jackets, called waistcoats, and bright red caps with long tassels.

The Oslo-Bergen railroad line is a tremendous engineering marvel. It has more than 200 tunnels (the longest is 3.25 miles, or 5.2 kilometers, long) and hundreds of miles of timber snowsheds. One of the most exciting train rides in the world is on the short line that climbs nearly 3,000 feet (912 meters) from the Flåm Valley.

Rather than reaching the summit by zigzagging, the train charges straight up the mountainside through a tunnel, emerging near the top beneath a gigantic waterfall, so close that its spray falls on the windows of the train.

Bergen

Bergen, Norway's second largest city (population 221,717), was for many years its largest, and many Bergensers are convinced that it is still the most important. Sitting in a maze of north-south fjords, it has a fine harbor, protected from ocean storms by a wall of low-lying islands. Founded in 1070 by King Olaf Kyrre, Bergen was for a time the royal capital, and later it was a Scandinavian outpost of the confederation of German cities known as the Hanseatic League. Until the days of air travel, it was Norway's window on the world and the starting point for any visit to the country.

Because of its long history of world trade, Bergen is more cosmopolitan than the rest of Norway. Bergen was the first city in Norway to have a symphony orchestra, and the National Academy of Science began here. Bergen also has the country's oldest theater. Called Den National Scene, it was founded in 1850 by the celebrated violinist Ole Bull (1810–80), one of Bergen's favorite sons.

Another world-renowned Bergenser was Norway's greatest composer, Edvard Grieg (1843–1907). He built an immense house, which

Elements of Norwegian folk music appear in many of composer Edvard Grieg's works, particularly in the music he wrote to accompany Peer Gynt, *a play by renowned Norwegian playwright Henrik Ibsen.*

The people of Bergen are proud of how their city (Norway's second largest) has maintained its traditions. The timber buildings and wharf, which have been rebuilt and preserved, still dominate the center of the city as they did when the ships of the Hanseatic League used to dock there.

he called Troldhaugen (Hill of Trolls) by Lake Nordas, south of the city. Today Troldhaugen is a Grieg museum. Each May, Bergen hosts the International Festival of Music, Drama, and Folklore in his honor.

To the north is the site of the original settlement (after one of its periodic fires, the city was rebuilt in its present location). To the south are newly built suburbs and industrial parks. Behind Floyen to the east, Bergen's hills rise to the Hardangervidda. Directly in front is the center of the city, including the ancient Hansa quay where the trading vessels of the Hanseatic League once docked. The tall, narrow warehouses of the Hansa are crowded closely along the quay. They seem to lean toward each other across the narrow street, and their gables overshadow the lower floors so that the offices need lamps even during the day. The longer modern piers jutting into Puddle Fjord are lined with freighters and fishing boats.

The central part of Bergen is a jumble of narrow, twisting streets overlaid by a grid of broad, straight avenues. Those avenues, called *almenninger*, are fire protection lanes. Like most cities in a country that has always built with wood, Bergen has suffered from fire several times; it was also heavily damaged during World War II. When the Bergensers rebuilt, they made sure that fire equipment would always be able to move quickly through the city. Today old and shabby buildings sit next to new ones, all brightened by the Norwegian love of color.

Stavanger

The last of the great east-west fjords is Bokno, and Stavanger lies inside its southern entrance. With 103,496 inhabitants, it is Norway's fourth largest city. Primarily because of the North Sea oil fields, it is also the country's fastest-growing city. Heliports, tankers, and multistory office buildings all show how much wealth and energy is being created in the stormy offshore waters. These symbols, or symptoms, of the rush for modernization stand in uneasy contrast to the cobblestone streets and old wooden buildings near the waterfront.

As the main city of Norway's conservative southwest, Stavanger is home to many members of the fundamentalist Lutheran and dissenting Protestant sects. Before it attracted an international community of workers in business suits and hard hats, it was famous as a city of churches. One cathedral is 800 years old, and a principal street, Berglandsgate (-*gate* means "street"), is lined with an amazing variety of churches, temples, and chapels.

Stavanger is also oil rich and cosmopolitan and boasts an equally rich variety of nightclubs, discos, and theaters in addition to expensive shops, gourmet restaurants, and outdoor cafés. The sandy beaches south of the city have become a summer playground for all of Scandinavia. Sometimes it seems that there are two very different cities, each called Stavanger. One is old and old-fashioned, and the other is modern and stylish.

A carefully restored building in Lillehammer on the shores of Lake Mjösa demonstrates how farmers in eastern Norway have long relied on forests as well as fields to survive.

Eastern Norway and Oslo

Eastern Norway has the gentlest landscape in Norway: rolling hills, broad green valleys, and sparkling lakes. Summers are sunnier and warmer than on the west coast. But the winters are colder, and the frost stays later in spring and comes earlier in fall. Snow covers the ground for at least three months of the year.

On the whole, though, nature is kinder here than in the rest of Norway. As a result, eastern Norway has always been the most populous region. It is also the richest. Half of Norway's arable land is in eastern Norway, and 55 percent of the country's forest resources are located here, mostly in the Hedmark region between the Glåma River and Sweden.

The Glåma is Norway's longest (372 miles, or 600 kilometers) and most important river. It rises on the Rörosvidda and runs south through the fir, spruce, and pine forests of Hedmark, then down through the fertile valley called Österdalen.

In winter the farmers of Österdalen become the lumberjacks of Hedmark. They fell trees and sled them to the sides of frozen mountain streams. Until recently, the loggers had to stay in the forests all winter. It was a very rough life. They spent the short winter day doing backbreaking, dangerous work and the long, cold nights huddled in primitive wooden huts, far from home and family. Today, Österdalen farmers still augment their income by logging in the upland forests. But chain saws and bulldozers ease the work a bit, and snowmobiles have ended the winter isolation.

In spring the loggers send the logs down streams swollen with melted snow to the Glåma. There workers assemble the logs into huge rafts, called booms, and float them downstream to the sawmills and paper mills of Sarpsborg.

Sarpsborg is part of a ring of industrial towns around Oslo Fjord. Besides the vast Borregaard Paper Mills, Sarpsborg's most impressive attraction is the river. In the center of town, the Glåma pours over a broad, 66-foot (22-meter) drop, surely one of the world's biggest municipal waterfalls.

A few miles downstream, past Frederikstad, the Glåma empties into Oslo Fjord. Frederikstad, destroyed several times by Swedish invaders, is a thriving industrial center filled with many remnants of its fighting past in addition to its modern lumber mills, anchovy canneries, food-processing plants, and a busy port. Earth and stone ramparts from the 17th century surround the Old Town. In front of these walls stands the grim stone fortress of Kongsten. East of Österdalen is Gudbrandsdalen, another inland valley. It is drained by the Lågen River, which flows into Lake Mjösa, the largest lake in Norway. Lillehammer, at the head of the lake, is a dramatically beautiful town. To the northeast the forests of Hedmark sweep up Kjölen in dark green waves. To the northwest the mountains of Oppland loom over the lake, and behind them glimmer the icecaps of Jotunheimen. Ski trails are vertical white scars on the rocky or tree-covered mountainsides.

At the southern end of the lake is the village of Eidsvold, a national shrine. It was there in 1814 that elected representatives of the people of Norway declared Norwegian independence and drafted the Norwegian constitution. Although Norway did not win full in-

At Eidsvold, a gathering of elected delegates met and drew up Norway's constitution, which they proclaimed on May 17, 1814. The constitution was based on democratic elements from the U.S., French, and Spanish constitutions.

dependence from Sweden for almost 100 years, Eidsvold is revered by every patriotic Norwegian as the cradle of Norwegian liberty.

Valdres, Hallingdal, and Numedal are shorter valleys to the west. They are drained by rivers that descend from the Long Mountains and empty into Oslo Fjord or the Skagerrak. Along their sides are farms, each with a path leading to a vidda pasture. As each valley descends to the lowlands surrounding Oslo and Oslo Fjord, the villages get larger, the roads get better, and the signs of industry and commerce increase.

But there is no sharp line between country and city. Many of the towns in the urbanized ring around Oslo have a rural air, and the city itself has been called "an overgrown country town."

Oslo

Between 1624 and 1877, Oslo was called Christiana, after a former Danish king. In 1878 it became Kristiana, but in 1925 it reverted to Oslo, its original name.

The city planners have gone to great lengths to preserve the natural beauty of Oslo. City limits enclose 175 square miles (453 square kilometers) at the northern end of Oslo Fjord, 60 miles (96 kilometers) from the Skagerrak. The built-up section of Oslo, however, takes up only 60 square miles (156 square kilometers). The

The Holmenkollen ski jump is just outside the crowded capital city of Oslo in the Oslomarka, easily reached by city dwellers in search of outdoor fun.

rest is a belt of pine-clad hills, lakes, and marshes that surrounds the city core. Called the Oslomarka (Oslo Field), it is dedicated to the open-air enjoyments that Norwegians love so much. There are picnic grounds, hiking and ski trails, and, of course, a ski jump. Canoes, windsurfers, and sailboats share the waters of Oslo Fjord with freighters, trawlers, and timber barges. Building in the Oslomarka is severely restricted, and no new construction is allowed to the north of the central city.

The city itself is handsome and constructed on a human scale. Homes, stores, and offices of many ages and architectural styles stand close together. Avenues of large stone houses from the 19th century give way to narrow alleys lined with wooden warehouses and shops that seem to date back to the 17th century. There are no skyscrapers, although there are several modern glass-and-steel office blocks. The twin brick towers of the monumental city hall rise over the waterfront.

Akershus Fortress looms over the harbor, near where the Akers River rushes into the fjord. Built in 1300, the fortress is Norway's largest. No longer needed as a defense against Danish or Swedish invasion, it is used as a museum and for some state ceremonies.

The stately Karl Johansgate runs east-west a few blocks back from the waterfront. Only about a mile (1.6 kilometers) long, it is nevertheless the city's main thoroughfare. It begins at the central railway station and ends at the royal palace, whose park offers a cloud of lilac blossoms in the spring and a lively toboggan run in the winter. Between these two landmarks are the national theater, the parliament building, and the Aula, or Great Hall, of Oslo University.

Oslo's *domkirken* (cathedral) is just off Karl Johansgate, behind the flower market. In contrast to the bright blossoms of the market, this dark building looks somber, but inside it is light and airy. The ceilings are covered with brilliant frescoes, painted after World War II, which illustrate the eternal battle between the forces of good and evil.

Blocks of small wooden houses line the narrow streets on the hillsides between the Karl Johansgate and the northern green belt. They were erected late in the 19th century, in what were then the outskirts of Oslo, to house workers. Today they are high-priced city dwellings for executives and young professionals.

Across the harbor from City Hall is Bygdöy Peninsula, where five museums celebrate Norway's proud heritage of seafarers and explorers. The Viking Ship Museum houses three 9th-century Viking longboats, slender wooden ships with masts and rowers' benches. Boats such as these were used by the Vikings to roam the seas and explore the streams and rivers of three continents.

Many of the stores, offices, homes, and historic landmarks of Oslo cluster along the street called Karl Johansgate.

The dashing Fridtjof Nansen was not only an accomplished explorer and oceanographer but also curator of the Museum of Natural History in Bergen, a university professor, the first Norwegian minister to Great Britain, and leader of Norway's first delegation to the League of Nations.

The museum's boats are actually funeral vessels, excavated from burial mounds along the shores of Oslo Fjord. Each contained the body of a Viking chieftain, along with his weapons, jewelry, horses, and other wealth. The boats and their contents are remarkably well preserved and offer tantalizing glimpses into a vanished world of rugged adventure and splendor.

In the Framhut, a huge building with the tent shape of an old Viking boathouse, the *Fram* sits in permanent dry dock. From 1893 to 1896 this sturdy boat, deliberately trapped in drifting polar ice, carried Fridtjof Nansen and his crew closer to the North Pole than any human had ever gone. Otto Sverdrup later used the *Fram* to explore and map the coast of Greenland. Finally the gallant sailing vessel carried Roald Amundsen to Antarctica for his successful race to be first to the South Pole.

Near the Framhut is the Kon Tiki Museum. The *Kon Tiki* is a balsa raft, built with primitive tools, containing no metal parts. In 1947, Norwegian explorer Thor Heyerdahl amazed and charmed the world by sailing the *Kon Tiki* 5,000 miles (8,000 kilometers) across the Pacific from Peru to Polynesia. The museum also houses the *Ra II*, a boat made of the African reed called papyrus, in which

Heyerdahl later sailed from Morocco to Barbados. Heyerdahl's expeditions were meant to prove that people from South American and African cultures could have traveled over the world's oceans before the European Age of Discovery. Norway honors him, however, for what he demonstrated about Norwegian courage, ingenuity, and stamina.

Oslo's central city is too small to house everyone who works and lives in Oslo. The harbor, with 8 miles (13 kilometers) of waterfront, is the country's busiest. Two-thirds of Norway's wholesale business and 50 percent of all retail trade are conducted in Oslo. Almost 30 percent of the industrial wages earned in Norway are earned, or paid out, in Oslo.

In the 1950s and 1960s, suburbs shot up west of the city center, and apartment buildings spread throughout the city, until city planners applied the brakes. Things were getting more and more crowded. The open spaces so beloved by Norwegians were disappearing. Although one could still ski almost into the center of the city, the water in the inner harbor became too dirty for safe swimming.

In the award-winning book named for his raft Kon Tiki, *Thor Heyerdahl described how he and his crew survived encounters with flying fish, giant whale sharks, and fierce storms as they crossed the Pacific Ocean in their raft of balsa, now in the Kon Tiki Museum.*

To lessen the crowding and allow for growth, Oslo has spread out. Industries were encouraged to move to industrial parks along both the east and west shores of Oslo Fjord. Apartment blocks and housing projects rose in satellite towns and bedroom communities east of Oslo. Today, although the population of Oslo itself has settled at around half a million, the surrounding Oslo metropolitan district contains more than 900,000 residents.

Fortunately, Oslo has a good public transportation system. Electric commuter rail lines run along both shores of the fjord and into the city in underground tunnels. There is a subway as well, and a fleet of shiny blue trolleys operates within city limits. Car ferries supplement the web of new highways in the region, and thousands of commuters beat rush-hour traffic by skimming to and from work on hydrofoil boats.

Telemark and the South Coast

Just a few miles west of the crowded, bustling Oslo Fjord district is the deep quiet of the Telemark region. Ancient farms nestle in secluded valleys under the Hardangervidda. Long, narrow lakes stretch along the shoulders of the mountains, and wild rivers rip through ravines so deep and narrow that sunlight never reaches the water.

Quieter rivers serve as highways for logs from Telemark's pine forests. Aside from Österdalen, Telemark produces more lumber and pulpwood than any other region. There are several large hydroelectric plants. At the Tokke plant near the town of Dalen, engineers channeled an entire waterfall into a tunnel, where it spins turbines that can produce 400,000 kilowatts.

Tourists are drawn by well-developed ski resorts and the lure of history. According to Telemarkers, skiing was invented here. Rude wooden skis from 2,500 years ago have been found in the area, so they are probably right. The region will always be connected with cross-country skiing because of the telemark turn, the characteristic maneuver that allows people on narrow skis in light, flexible shoes to carve swooping turns down all but the steepest slopes.

During World War II, Norwegian resistance fighters used their skiing and mountaineering skills in a daring act of sabotage that crippled the Nazi effort to develop an atomic bomb. The Germans were using a hydroelectric plant in the remote valley of Vemork to produce "heavy water," water enriched with radioactive isotopes that was crucial to their experiments. Skiing silently past the German troops surrounding the site, the Norwegians climbed into the snow-filled gorge one dark night and destroyed the plant with dynamite charges.

In the rugged highlands to the west is Setesdal, eastern Norway's most isolated valley. The Otra River winds along the floor of the steep valley. Where rockfall has created natural dams, the river widens to form lakes. At Byglands Fjord the lake completely fills the valley floor. Along both shores the mountains rise straight out of the water—rock walls hundreds of feet high. Not even a mountain climber could enter or leave the valley at the lake's lower end.

Traditional farms remain tucked into the sheltered valleys of Telemark.

Setesdal is easier to reach now that a tunnel over a third of a mile long pierces the mountain and connects the upper valley with Kristiansand at the mouth of the Otra. Because of its long isolation, however, the region has an old-fashioned air. The farmers look oddly formal in their traditional black trousers, white shirts, and narrow-brimmed black felt hats. Women work in the fields, raking hay and hanging it to dry like laundry on wooden frames. They dress in black stockings, white woolen skirts, and short black or red jackets over white blouses. Married women cover their head with a scarf that frames their face like a bonnet and hangs down their back like pigtails.

On Sunday, the women put black skirts and blouses over the white ones to go to church. For festive occasions, such as weddings, they wear yet another overskirt, of red. The men wear black trousers with leather seats and brightly colored cuffs and pullover smocks decorated with matching colors.

Downstream, the Otra River flows to the sea through Kristiansand, the predominant town of a completely different region. This is Sörlandet, or South Land, Norway's Riviera.

On Sundays in isolated Setesdal, some young Norwegians, such as this little girl, proudly wear their distinctive embroidered outfits to church services.

This stretch of coast along the Skagerrak is not as lush or hot as the Riviera beaches along the Mediterranean, but it is warmer than Norway's other coasts. In summer the relatively warm water and the sandy beaches attract sun worshipers from all over Norway and from Sweden and Denmark as well. Thousands of vacation homes, ranging from simple huts to snug cabins, dot the belt of skerries along the coast. Many were once the year-round dwellings of fishing families.

Lillesand, Grimstad, Arendal, Tvedestrand—a branch of the coastal rail line connects this string of lovely towns running up the shore north of Kristiansand. Once fishing villages, they now are summer resorts and the permanent home of artists and craftspeople. Red-roofed white cottages, each with its patch of garden and each facing in a different direction, line the alleys that corkscrew up the rocky slopes. Higher, the handsome homes built by ship captains and traders recall the prosperous days of the sea, when the region's merchant fleet was the country's largest.

Rail service is by autocar, a single car like a trolley that runs along the shore. Passengers can sit next to the driver and chat as it rolls through the gentle scenery, stopping on request by a country doorstep or path leading to the beach.

Inland, the main rail line connecting Oslo and Kristiansand is a much more impressive feat of engineering. The tracks run along the shoulders of mountains and cross deep gorges on graceful steel spans. Where there is no way around, they disappear into tunnels blasted through the mountain's heart. This stretch of railroad was one of the most expensive, per mile, ever built. It also provides one of the most exciting train rides on earth.

The image of the bold Viking warrior has captured the imagination of writers and artists since Norsemen first swept down from Scandinavia to conquer and loot the coastal settlements of northern Europe in the 9th century.

Norway's History

Stone Age hunter-gatherers wandered into Norway at the end of the last Ice Age, some 11,000 years ago. Because so much water was still locked up in the glaciers, the oceans were low, and there was probably a land bridge between present-day Denmark and the Scandinavian Peninsula.

For many centuries, the north was far warmer than it is now. Forests covered much of the land, and there was plenty of plant and animal food for the settlers. Gradually, however, the air cooled, the tree line retreated south, and foraging for food became much harder.

As it often does, hardship stirred ingenuity. Under the pressure of hunger, people learned to make better tools, to hunt more effectively, and to save seeds from plants that they gathered and sow them in the spring. Agriculture began in the narrow strips of soil beside the fjords and on the rocky coastal plain. The plows of today's Norwegian farmers sometimes turn up the shaped pieces of stone that their ancestors used as axes and digging sticks. The tools from this period show that their makers had learned to polish the rough edges of the chipped stone, which made them sharper and longer lasting. This was a crucial development in human technology, and it gave its name to the period, which archaeologists call the Neolithic, or New Stone Age.

Because of the scanty soil and short growing season, the inhabitants of ancient Norway kept their hunting and foraging skills even as they learned how to farm. If the crops failed, they could still fall back on the bounty of the sea, for instance, or trap forest animals for food.

As their civilization progressed, the lives of these early Norwegians became easier. Trade developed among the tribes along the coast and between those tribes and more advanced peoples to the south. We know this because prehistoric people buried the bodies of their leaders in earthen mounds, called barrows, and surrounded them with their tools, clothing, and decorations. Archaeologists can tell much about vanished cultures by looking at the contents of their tombs.

Another source of information about the early Norwegians is their rock carvings and paintings, found on cliffs on the southern and western coasts. This evidence shows that these people worshiped several gods, including the sun, which is represented by a disk in a wheeled cart. Some paintings in nearby Sweden hint that the religious practices there included human sacrifice. We do know that human sacrifice was a feature of the later Viking religion until as late as the 7th or 8th century A.D.

Around 2000 B.C., tools and jewelry made of bronze began to appear in Scandinavia. Bronze, a mixture of copper and tin, is an easily worked metal that makes stronger weapons and tools than either bone or stone. Like the ability to make stone tools, the ability to make bronze was an important advance in civilization, and the period following its introduction is called the Bronze Age. The Bronze Age came late to Scandinavia, because the necessary tin and copper do not occur near the surface there. When bronze came to Norway, it came in the hands of invading tribes of tall, fair-haired people from the east. These Germanic or Nordic tribes, called Aryans, overran the more primitive inhabitants and took possession of their farms and villages. Their descendants are today's Norwegians.

Once settled, the new inhabitants continued the process of turning stony fields into farms. Fishing was still important, and boat-building skills improved. The Norwegians developed boats that could be rowed or powered by a primitive sail. During this period their fishing and trade voyages were still confined to the protected waters of the way northward.

There was, however, a busy overland trade to the south. Norwegian fur and amber (fossilized tree resin) were traded for tools, weapons, pottery, and glass. Coins found in graves from the Bronze Age show that the trade reached to the Greek and Roman civilizations of the Mediterranean.

Trade with the south began to fall off, however, around 500 B.C. The world climate had taken another turn, and the Northern Hemisphere became much colder. This change caused great migrations and conflicts as nomadic tribes again swept from the plains of Russia across Europe in search of better food supplies. The nomads pushed the already settled tribes west, and these displaced tribes in turn displaced people settled there, until all Europe was in upheaval. Besides the interruption of trade, Scandinavia suffered directly from the change in weather. Population declined as crops failed, and many villages slipped back into the hunting way of life.

Strangely, the first description of Norway written by a foreign visitor dates from this period of isolation. In the Mediterranean, Alexander the Great was preparing to conquer the world. To him, the world stretched away south and east, and he marched in those directions. But in 330 B.C. a Greek from Marseilles named Pytheas sailed along the coast of Britain to the small islands north of Britain. Legend had told him of a land at the end of the earth called Ultima Thule, and he sailed northeast to find it.

Anthropologists believe these stone inscriptions found outside Trondheim depict a Bronze Age religious procession. The small figures above the stick figures may be gods; the circles with crosses represent the sun.

What he found was the west coast of Norway, where he spent the summer. Like all tourists, Pytheas was entranced by the midnight sun. He reported that the people were more primitive and had coarser food than in the south. They lived on wild fruit, roots, vegetables, and oats. It must have been an unlucky season for the hunters.

In time, stability returned and trade between Norway and the south resumed, mainly because of the Romans. By the end of the 1st century A.D. their empire had expanded to the Rhine River in central Europe, and they were carrying on extensive trade along the coast of the North Sea. Roman traders introduced the two most important innovations of the next thousand years to Norway: iron and writing.

Humans had first learned to smelt iron about 3000 B.C. The Iron Age, marked by widespread use of this metal, had begun around 1500 B.C. in the Middle East. The technology of iron did not reach northern and western Europe until 500 B.C., and iron was still very little known in Scandinavia when the Romans brought it.

Once it arrived, iron made revolutionary changes in war, agriculture, and shipbuilding. Iron swords and spears gave men an advantage over those using the softer bronze. Iron-shod plows, sickles, and axes greatly increased agricultural production, which led to population growth, trade, and surplus wealth. These developments led, over time, to a more complex social system, including the creation of a class of war leaders, called *jarls*.

Soon Norwegians began importing iron in ingots and making their own implements. They particularly excelled in jewelry or ornamentation of filigree and in inlaid decorations of gold and silver set in iron. The most important development was the discovery that Norway abounded in deposits, near the surface, of easily smelted iron ore called bog iron.

Before long, every farmer was also a smith. Large areas of forest were cut down to produce charcoal, which was necessary for the smelting process. An ironworking industry began to develop. According to the archaeological evidence, by the 9th century A.D. a humble farmstead in Norway had more iron implements than a large manor belonging to Charlemagne, the Holy Roman Emperor.

The effect of iron on shipbuilding was also immense. With iron axes, shipbuilders could make planks, which make much more seaworthy boats than do logs. A 7th-century boat excavated from a mound at Kvalsund is 50 feet (15 meters) long, with slender lines, a raised prow and stern, a keel, and a rudder. This early version of

Fierce-looking animal heads decorated the prows (fronts) of Viking longboats, but even more frightening were the Vikings themselves. Their whirlwind raids terrorized coastal villagers.

the Viking longboat shows that by the end of the Roman Empire, the Norwegians already had the ability to roam the oceans.

The second great contribution of the Romans was writing. All the inhabitants of Scandinavia spoke a common language, and they adapted the Roman alphabet to it. Because they lacked paper or parchment, most of their writing took the form of inscriptions on stone and wood markers, made with a knife or ax. The letters, called runes, therefore consisted entirely of straight lines that could be carved easily.

The Viking Age

With the decline of the Roman Empire in the 6th century, war in western Europe interrupted trade, and Scandinavia retreated from Europe. This time, however, civilization did not falter in Norway.

Communities grew. Small tribes merged into larger tribes, and what was to become known as Viking society developed. There were freedmen who worked their own farms, servants (called thralls) who were bound to the farm and worked for the freedmen, and jarls who protected the communities and led them in battles and raids. By the 9th century, when the Viking raids began, what is now Norway was a loose confederation of small kingdoms, well organized, vigorous, and with energy to burn. To the astonished inhabitants of northern Europe, they were savages, barbarians, maybe demons from hell. After the spring plowing and the fall harvest, the men of Scandinavia would go *a'viking* (raiding). The Norwegians sailed south and west to plunder Irish monasteries and Scottish villages. The Danes slipped down the English Channel to raid the coasts of France and England. The Swedes sailed across the Baltic and down Russia's Dnieper and Volga rivers as far as Constantinople.

Slipping up a tidal creek, the Vikings would leap from their ship and fall upon unsuspecting villagers, cutting down any who opposed them. They seized women and children as slaves, took everything of value that they could get into the ship, and sometimes burned the rest.

According to the legend, Erik the Red was exiled from Iceland for killing an Icelandic chief, as shown in this old engraving. Whatever the reason, Erik certainly left Iceland in 982 and founded Norwegian colonies in Greenland.

The Viking Age was not just banditry, however. It was the outward expansion of a vigorous culture. For the Danes, the yearly raids in northern England gave way to settlement. For a time, the Danes ruled half of England and took a yearly tribute in gold, called the Danegeld, to refrain from attacking the other half.

Raids were succeeded by invasion in France, where the Norwegian chieftain Rollo led a Viking army up the Seine River and threatened Paris. To save the city, the French king gave the invaders rich land in western France. The land given to the Norsemen was called Normandy, and Rollo became the first duke of Normandy. One hundred and fifty years later, Rollo's descendant, William of Normandy, successfully invaded England and became its king.

The Norwegian Vikings also conquered the Isle of Man, the Hebrides Islands, and most of Ireland. In 1066 they invaded southern England, where they were repelled at the Battle of Stamford Bridge. It was this invasion, many believe, that weakened the English forces and led to their defeat by William at Hastings later that summer. In any case, from then on the ruling classes of both England and France were descended from Norwegian Vikings.

Besides raids and invasions, the Norwegian Vikings made voyages of discovery and colonization. In 870 they established settlements in Iceland. In 985, Erik the Red brought the first group of settlers to Greenland, which a storm-blown Viking had discovered a century earlier. Greenland's name was either an early public relations trick or a bitter joke, for the huge island is permanently covered in ice, except for a single fertile valley and a narrow strip of land along the west coast. The colony survived, mostly on trade in walrus hides and ivory, for more than 400 years, then failed when trade with Norway was interrupted by war and plague in Europe.

In 1000, Erik the Red's son, Leif Eriksson, roamed far to the west and found a fertile coast that he named Vinland. The next year he returned with several ships and founded a colony. Things went well at first, but turmoil in the ranks and hostile natives caused the Vikings to abandon the colony. Nordic sagas, or poems of history and legend, preserved some references to the lost Vinland colony.

For years, the location of Vinland was hotly disputed. Many believed that Vinland was in North America and that a bold Norwegian had discovered America 492 years before the Genoan Christopher Columbus. There was no proof, however. The Vikings did not have extensive written records. What we know of Viking history comes from their sagas, long narrative poems that were recited by Nordic bards and handed down from generation to generation. It was hundreds of years before anyone thought of writing them down. By that time, it was impossible to separate fact from fiction. Because no trace of Viking settlement had been found in North America, those who argued that the Norwegians discovered America had few facts to back them up.

In 1963, however, Norwegian archaeologist Helge Instad discovered the ruins of nine earthen structures and a smithy on the Canadian island of Newfoundland. The building methods were definitely Viking, and carbon dating showed that the site was occupied around the year 1000. This may not have been Leif Eriksson's Vinland colony, but Instad's discovery proved at last that Vikings had indeed reached America long before any other European.

To European Christians, the Vikings were godless pagans, but in fact they worshiped many gods. Chief was Odin, or Wotan, father of the gods, whose wife was named Frigga. Thor was the god of war; his weapons were a hammer and a thunderbolt. Frey was the god of fertility, Freya the goddess of love and beauty. Remnants of the Viking gods persist in the names of the week: Wednesday, Thursday, and Friday were named for, respectively, Odin (Wotan), Thor, and Freya.

Norway Becomes a Nation

Even as the Vikings were shaking up Europe, their raids, conquests, and expanded trade were reshaping their own society. Along with slaves and loot, their ships brought back new ideas and new ways of looking at things. Two of the most powerful new notions they acquired were nationhood and Christianity.

When the Norwegian Vikings first besieged Europe, each band came from one of several small kingdoms along the coast. Each band was loyal to its leader and to no one else, and the bands were quick to raid each other if opportunity existed. Soon, however, the bands learned to act together in order to mount bigger raids or invasions. About 900, Harald Hårfager (Fairhair) defeated several small kingdoms and persuaded others to accept his leadership. He became Harald I, first king of the newly unified nation of Norway. Toward the end of the 10th century, King Olaf I Tryggvason introduced Christianity to Norway. Vikings were usually tolerant of other religions, but many fiercely resisted giving up their old gods, as the priests of the new religion demanded. Partly because of this resistance, the young kingdom of Norway splintered.

In 1015, King Olaf II Haraldson reunified the country and established Christianity as the state religion. Olaf II was overthrown by Canute, the Danish king of England, who invaded Norway in 1028 and was a fierce supporter of the old Viking religion and ways. In 1030, Olaf II was killed in battle as he tried to regain his throne. Ironically, Olaf's death accomplished what he could not achieve in

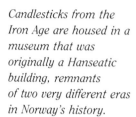

Candlesticks from the Iron Age are housed in a museum that was originally a Hanseatic building, remnants of two very different eras in Norway's history.

life. His subjects were inspired by his martyrdom and resentful of foreign invasion. Within a generation, the entire country had converted to the new religion, and Olaf had been declared Norway's patron saint.

By the end of the 11th century, with the triumph of Christianity and the establishment of strong kingdoms throughout Europe, the Viking Age was over. In Norway, cities such as Bergen, Stavanger, and Trondheim became important trading centers. Oslo was founded in 1050 by King Harald Hardraade (Hard Ruler) as a military outpost to protect against Danish invasion.

The Norwegian monarchy was never strictly hereditary—that is, kingship did not simply pass from father to son. To claim the kingship, a leader had to establish his personal power and win the approval of the ting. After 1130, rival claims to the throne led to a series of civil wars among the regions. The wars and a string of bad harvests caused grain shortages that led the country deep into debt to the merchant rulers of the Hanseatic League, a group of northern German trading cities bound together by treaties of mutual protection. By 1300, Bergen was a Hansa town, and the rest of the country was largely controlled by the league, which gained sole trading rights in Scandinavia in 1370.

Union with Denmark

In 1349 and 1350, Norway was first struck by the Black Death, or bubonic plague. At least one-third of the country's half million inhabitants died. In 1380 the weakened country was united with Denmark under Margaret, widow of King Haakon VI, who was also queen of Denmark. In 1388, Margaret was invited by the Swedes to become their monarch also. Finally, Margaret united the three countries in 1397 under the Union of Kalmar, which established separate national governments but gave the greatest share of power to Denmark.

Neither Norway nor Sweden was happy with this arrangement for long. Sweden made several attempts to leave the union and regained its independence after a bloody revolt in 1523. Norway, on the other hand, became progressively weaker and in 1536 lost its national government and became a province of Denmark. At the same time Denmark made Lutheranism the official religion.

During the 16th century, Norway's lumber was in great demand all over Europe. The country's shipping industry began a period of growth that would make the industry, by the 18th century, one of the world's largest.

The shifting alliances between European nations during the Napoleonic Wars in the late 18th and early 19th centuries affected Scandinavia greatly. Even though Britain was Norway's chief trading

The sagas, or epic poems, of the Vikings were told and retold in homes such as these reconstructed Viking buildings near Oslo.

partner, Denmark sided with France against Britain. Britain's warships then blockaded Norwegian ports, preventing trade with other countries. The blockade was so effective that many Norwegians starved. Yet it also separated Norway from Denmark, allowing the Norwegians to resume control of their country. They also secretly resumed trade with Britain.

The Treaty of Kiel

Sweden was a British ally from the start. The Swedes defeated Danish forces in 1813; the following year, the Treaty of Kiel forced the Danes to give up Norway to Sweden. However, Denmark kept Norway's colonies: Iceland, Greenland, and the Faeroe Islands. These great-power maneuvers were unacceptable to the people of Norway. After 400 years of rule by Denmark, the last thing they wanted was Swedish domination. They were also angered by the loss of their colonies. In May 1814, elected representatives of the Norwegian people met at Eidsvold and declared Norway's independence. They also wrote and adopted a constitution that called for the combination of a hereditary monarchy (which was offered to a Danish prince) and parliamentary democracy.

The Swedes were not impressed with Norway's call for liberty and freedom. They moved quickly to take control of their trophy of war. Sweden decisively defeated Norway in several skirmishes, and in September 1814, the parliament accepted the king of Sweden as ruler of Norway. For his part, the Swedish king promised to respect the Norwegian constitution.

Norway's shotgun marriage with Sweden was for the most part peaceful, although the Norwegian parliament struggled continually for real power over the affairs of the nation. For example, the parliament demanded the right to control cabinet ministers—the people who administer the day-to-day affairs of government. That right was not won until 1884.

(continued on p. 89)

SCENES OF
NORWAY

◄ A waterfall rushing down the slopes of Sogne Fjord is a breathtaking sight, but Norway's waterfalls provide more than scenery—they also provide clean, cheap hydroelectric power.

◄ *In the far north of Norway a few Samí continue their nomadic way of life, following their reindeer herds across the tundra. Today, however, their homes are more likely to be small houses than reindeer hide tents.*

▼ *Norway is home to Europe's largest ice field, located on the Jostedalsbreen plateau. The Boya glacier, part of the huge field, spreads down to the waters of Fjaerlands Fjord.*

➤ *In a secluded valley northwest of the cosmopolitan city of Bergen a small wooden church lies nestled near the Flam River.*

⋁ *The heart of Bergen, long a center of world trade, is its harbor. Hanseactic warehouses line the waterfront; behind them, hills rise to the Hardangervidda.*

⋏ *Mountains, forests, farms, and water—nearly all the elements that compose the Norwegian countryside—are part of the scenery on the way to the resort town of Molde.*

⋏ *The Holmenkollen ski jump in the Oslomarka is a center of outdoor fun in summer as well as winter.*

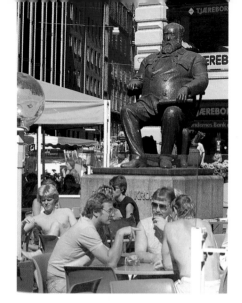

➤ *Norwegians enjoy the warm summer weather in an outdoor café in the capital city of Oslo.*

◄ *On weekends, downtown Trondheim features a colorful market where the abundant fruits and vegetables of the surrounding Trondelag region are displayed for city shoppers.*

⋏ *Model-airplane enthusiasts enjoy a view of the bridge linking Tromsö to the mainland from the slopes above the city.*

(continued from p. 80)

The rest of the 19th century saw steady growth in Norway's cities. There were economic upturns and downswings, but in general trade and industry increased. The system of roads grew slowly—building roads in Norway's mountains is a difficult and expensive process even today. In 1854 the country's first railroad, between Oslo and Eidsvold, was completed. By the end of the century it would extend all the way to Trondheim, and in 1909 the Oslo-Bergen line finally tied together eastern and western Norway.

As improvements in transportation opened up the valleys, isolated farms and villages gained access to the modern world. Farm prices, rural education, and the quality of rural life improved—but only for a time. The rural population increased, but the available land did not. By the middle of the century, there were far too many people in Norway for the available land and jobs.

Norwegians proudly marched through the streets to celebrate their separation from Sweden in 1905. The push for Norwegian independence began in 1814, with the passage of the Norwegian constitution.

In response, thousands of young Norwegians once more left the crowded valleys and took to the ocean—this time as peaceful emigrants instead of warlike Vikings. They traveled to the United States and Canada to homestead on the plains. When no more good farmland was available there, they moved to the cities of the upper Midwest to work in meat-packing plants and steel mills. Emigration reached its peak in 1883, when 28,000 left to find new lives across the ocean. In the 100 years between 1825 and 1925, more than 800,000 Norwegians left the country.

Independence

In 1905, Norwegian discontent with the forced union with Sweden peaked. The Norwegian parliament passed a law creating a Norwegian foreign service, but the Swedish king vetoed the law (refused to pass it). On June 7 the parliament responded to this insult by ending the union.

Sweden was prepared to fight again to keep Norway but relented after a nationwide referendum in which practically every Norwegian voted for independence. The union was dissolved, and Norway elected as king the Danish prince Carl, who took the name King Haakon VII.

For people who pride themselves on their stiff-necked rejection of privilege and rank, the Norwegians' love for their king is surprising. During World War II, Haakon led the doomed resistance to the German invasion, then escaped to England at the last possible moment. From there he headed a government in exile that became the focus of the Norwegian underground resistance to Nazi occupation. In 1957, Haakon's son succeeded him as King Olaf V and remained on the throne until his death in 1991. His son, Harald V, succeeded him. Like his father, the current king fulfills his mostly ceremonial duties with dignity and charm. Recent public opinion polls show that a vast majority of Norwegians want to see the monarchy continue.

Prince Carl of Denmark (third from left, back row) accepted the throne of the newly independent kingdom of Norway in 1905 and was approved in a national election.

Industrialization, War, and Peace

By the year of independence, Norway had developed many new industries, including textiles and wood-pulp production. Older industries, such as stone quarrying and metal production, revived. In 1885 electricity was used in a factory for the first time. Over the next three decades, as hydroelectric power became cheaper and more available, the number of factory workers in the country doubled. Norway's shipping and logging industries continued to expand as well. And as the number of jobs increased, the standard of living rose.

Because the Industrial Revolution came late to Norway, it managed to escape some of the worst problems and abuses of the factory age. By the time industrialization reached Norway, the social problems that can be created by large-scale manufacturing had become obvious. Models for laws to protect child laborers, for example, already existed in other nations such as England. In addition, Norway's urban slums that housed factory workers were not as bad as those of England because many of Norway's new industries were located in the mountains, close to the source of hydroelectric power. A number of these factories were managed by the workers, so working conditions tended to be better than in other nations.

The working class, as a whole, was better educated and better organized in Norway than elsewhere. Labor unions and craft guilds arose in the 1880s, and in 1887 socialists formed the Labor party. Broadly speaking, socialists believe that the government, or the people in general, should own and control property so that all share equally in the goods and services that are produced. The Norwegian Labor party, however, believed in a more moderate, or partial, version of socialism. Even so, they did not elect a member to the Storting (parliament) until 1903.

Norway's economy flourished during World War I. The country was neutral, but because so much of its trade was with Britain, Norwegian ships were German targets. Almost 50 percent of the merchant fleet was sunk by German submarines or mines.

Like all industrial nations, Norway suffered greatly from the worldwide depression of the 1930s. Factories closed, and as many as one-third of Norway's workers were unemployed. People became dissatisfied, and the Labor party gained control in 1935 by forming a coalition government with the Farmer's party. (When no single party in a parliament has enough members to make a majority, two or more parties may agree to vote together as a coalition in order to gain a majority and control of the government.)

The new government made sweeping changes. It increased taxes and began a public works program that gave many people jobs and added greatly to the nation's systems of roads and power stations. The government also created an old-age pension plan that was the beginning of what is now one of the most complete social security programs in the world.

As World War II approached, Norway again declared itself neutral, but Germany attacked all the seaports at once on April 9, 1940. Norwegian resistance was stiff, but it could not withstand the Germans' ruthless bombing and troop superiority. On June 10 the king and government were evacuated by British commandos, and Norway surrendered.

The Germans installed a puppet government of Norwegians who would follow their orders. The prime minister was Vidkun Quisling, a Norwegian who had supported the Nazis before the war. After the war he was executed as a collaborator (someone who cooperates with a country's enemies), and his last name became an international byword: In many of the languages of the world, the word *quisling*

Born in 1903, King Olaf V ascended to the throne in 1957. He married Princess Martha of Sweden while he was still crown prince.

Vidkun Quisling (right) led the Norwegian government appointed by Adolf Hitler during the Nazi occupation in World War II. Thoroughly despised by many Norwegians, Quisling was executed at the war's end.

means "traitor." Large numbers of Norwegians continued to resist the Germans after the surrender. Some fled to England and joined the Allied armies. Both the Norwegian merchant fleet and the Norwegian navy helped the Allies, and by the war's end half of Norway's ships had been destroyed. Inside Norway, an underground resistance army was very active. Its members raided German installations and blew up vital trains and ships. After each raid, the Germans shot, tortured, or imprisoned many Norwegians, but the attacks continued. When the Germans retreated from northern Norway near the end of the war, they practiced the "scorched-earth" policy; every building in the county of Finnmark was burned to the ground.

After the war, Norway joined the United Nations as a charter member, just as it had joined the League of Nations after World War I. In 1949 a Norwegian, Trygve Lie, became the first secretary-general of the United Nations. Norway knew enough of war to be committed to the cause of peace, but Norway had also learned of the dangers of neutrality. That same year, the country became one of the first members of the North Atlantic Treaty Organization (NATO).

NATO is the military alliance between the Western European democracies, the United States, and Canada; together the member countries promote stability in Europe and undertake to defend members against military threats. For decades, Norwegian troops, planes, and ships have participated in NATO training exercises.

Norway rebounded strongly from the ruin caused by World War II. American aid and loans financed the rebuilding of plants, ships, and schools. In the 1950s and 1960s the steel and shipbuilding industries worked at full capacity as Europe rebuilt itself.

The worldwide economic slowdown, or recession, of the 1970s caused a temporary but severe setback in Norway. Steel and shipbuilding in particular suffered, and the fishing industry also declined. At the same time, however, the Norwegian economy was helped by the discovery of oil in the North Sea and by the growth of high technology and service industries.

Despite some further ups and downs, Norway's industry was running strong by the late 1990s. Norway continues to be one of the world leaders in oil exports. It also remains a major exporter of metals, such as magnesium and aluminum, whose production requires large amounts of energy. Other important industries serving the export market include chemicals, paper, and wood pulp.

Overall, Norway's export-driven industries remain primarily based on raw materials or "semiprocessed" goods (meaning, for instance, metal rather than automobiles). The government is still working to structure the economy to stimulate new and efficient industrial enterprises.

The elected legislators of the Storting, the Norwegian parliament, represent the voters in their district. This Samí appeared before a Storting session in which policies affecting the Samí were discussed.

Government and Economy

Norway is a constitutional monarchy and a parliamentary democracy. The king is the head of state but has little to do with the actual government of the country. According to the constitution, the queen cannot be head of state.

The Storting, Norway's parliament, makes the laws and decides on policies. There are 165 members, elected every 4 years. Each member is elected from and represents 1 of the country's 19 counties (called *fylker*). Each county elects from 4 to 15 members, according to population. Oslo, which is considered a county, elects 15 members; Finnmark, the least populous county, elects 4.

The Storting has only one house, unlike England's parliament, which has a House of Lords and a House of Commons, or the legislature of the United States, with its Senate and House of Representatives. When considering legislation, however, the Storting divides into two sections, the Odelsting and the Lagting. Each section must approve a bill before it can become law. In theory, the king can veto a bill by refusing to sign it. Since independence in 1905, however, this has never happened.

The leader of the party that has the most members in parliament usually becomes the prime minister, who is the head of the government. The cabinet, also called the council of state, administers the government. It consists of 17 ministers chosen by the prime minister. Cabinet members may not be members of the Storting.

Each minister heads a ministry, or government department. Ministries include agriculture, commerce and shipping, defense, finance, and fisheries, among others. Because the Norwegians are so concerned about the quality of their natural world, in 1972 they created the Ministry of the Environment to oversee and protect the country's natural resources.

Sometimes disputes arise between those who make the laws and those who administer them. If the Storting votes against the cabinet's wishes or policies on an important issue, the minister of the ministry concerned, or perhaps the whole cabinet, resigns.

The King of Norway officially opens a session of the Storting. The Storting meets annually on the first weekday of October and continues as long as necessary to resolve legislative matters.

*Gro Harlem Brundtland of the Labor
party became the first woman
prime minister of Norway in 1981.*

Every citizen 18 or older may vote, and a very high proportion
of them do. They choose among candidates backed by the political
parties. The largest parties are the Labor, Center, and Conservative
parties. There are several other parties as well, ranging from the
Christian People's party to the Socialist Left.

From 1935 to 1965 the Labor party was in power, sometimes
in coalition with the Farmer's party. Labor governments practiced a
moderate socialism, which has been called "the middle way" between
socialism and unregulated capitalism. Many new parties formed in
the late 1960s and the 1970s. In the late 1970s a coalition government headed by the Christian Democratic Appeal party came to
power. For most of the time since the late 1980s, another coalition — principally composed of Labor, Center, and Conservative parties — has governed.

Norway's 19 counties are divided into 454 municipalities. Each
municipality elects a council, which then elects a board of aldermen
and a mayor. Each municipal council collects taxes from the people
and businesses within its boundaries. These taxes are in addition to

federal taxes that people must pay to the national government. The municipal councils are responsible for schools, social and health services, roads, water, utilities, the fire-fighting service, and zoning. Delegates from the municipal councils make up county councils, which administer joint projects, such as roads and hospitals. County governors, appointed by the cabinet, lead the county councils.

The cabinet also appoints all judges, usually for life terms. The Supreme Court consists of a chief justice and 17 justices, although most Supreme Court sessions are held with only 5 justices. However, the entire court meets to decide questions of constitutional law.

Many cases never get to court because of the Norwegian belief in the good sense and wisdom of the average citizen. Each municipality elects three lay persons (meaning that they are not legal professionals) to a conciliation council. Every dispute that might go to a regular court is first brought before the council, which, with the guidance of one professional judge, tries to settle the matter without a trial. About one-third of all cases are settled this way.

In the same way, the Examining and Summary Court takes care of many criminal cases without the expense and bother of a full trial. Summary Court is presided over by one professional judge; there is no jury. Cases go to the Summary Court when the crime is not a major offense and the accused has confessed and agreed to accept the court's judgment.

Other criminal cases go before 1 of the 110 city or district courts, where a panel of 1 professional and 2 lay judges jointly decide on guilt and sentencing. Appeals go to the Supreme Court.

The most serious criminal charges (such as murder, rape, and large-scale narcotics dealing) go to one of the five high courts. A jury of 10 citizens decides guilt or innocence; its decision cannot be appealed. Then four members of the jury, selected by ballot, confer with three professional judges to pronounce sentence. The sentence can be appealed.

Norwegian prisons are not the stone lockups of an earlier day. Their purpose is not to punish but to rehabilitate. Prisoners live in homelike rooms instead of cells. Inmates with good records are allowed to go home on leave for as long as a month.

Norway is serious about national defense. The experience of World War II taught Norwegians to be prepared for invasion. Military service is required for all men and is voluntary for women. Regular service lasts from 12 to 15 months, with refresher training until age 44. The armed forces' peacetime strength is about 30,000, but the reserve and home guard forces are ready to be called up in case of emergency. In the event of war, Norway could quickly have 320,000 troops, about 8 percent of the population, under arms.

Norway has a small air force, well equipped with the latest in fighters, fighter-bombers, and antiaircraft missiles. The navy, specialized for defending the coast and escorting merchant ships, consists of 5 frigates, 2 corvettes (small armed warships), 14 submarines, and many small, fast patrol boats.

Of course, Norway's forces could not stop a full-scale invasion by a major power such as its large neighbor, Russia. That threat, which waxes and wanes with the changes in superpower relations, lies behind Norway's participation in NATO.

Prepared for war, Norway works for peace. Norwegian troops have been part of UN peacekeeping missions around the globe, including Africa and the Middle East.

Economic Policy

Norway's pursuit of moderate socialism has produced a mixed economy. Most businesses are privately owned, but certain major industries that are crucial to the economy—transportation, mining, the production of metals—are nationalized (that is, owned and run by the government). The rapidly growing oil industry operates under a mixture of private and state ownership. The government tries to limit

Oil drilling platforms (left) are assembled in Oslo harbor in front of City Hall (right). The government regulates the profitable oil industry but does not wholly own it.

foreign ownership of Norwegian companies, but a large part of the enormous investment needed to exploit the North Sea oil fields came from giant multinational oil companies.

The huge revenues from North Sea oil export play an important part in the Norwegian economy, and oil taxes are a significant source of revenue for the government. On the other hand, if oil prices slump, as they did in the 1980s, the economy may have problems.

Norway's socialist government is deeply involved in managing, not owning, the means of production. Agriculture, fishing, and lumbering, for instance, are not nationalized, but the government subsidizes them; that is, it supports them with public money. Most farms are smaller than 25 acres (10 hectares) but very productive; because of a shortage of farm labor, they are highly mechanized. Norwegian dairy products are exported all over the world.

Norway's farmers own two-thirds of the 16 million acres (6.48

million hectares) of productive forests. The wood-processing industry accounts for about 10 percent of the country's total earnings
from products sold abroad. That income is very welcome to the many
farmers who suffer from the high costs of operating farms and sometimes from low prices for their farm produce.

Fishing is still important to the farmers and to the country. It
provides about 60,000 jobs, most of them seasonal. Ninety percent of
the total catch is exported. The government also subsidizes the shipbuilding industry, which sagged in the 1980s but has rebounded
since. Norway still controls about 10 percent of the world's commercial fleet.

Norway's railroads are state owned and usually run at a loss.
The cost of building and maintaining track in such mountainous
terrain is astronomical. Two lines connect Oslo and Trondheim, and
there are several east-west lines, including lines between Bergen and
Oslo and Stavanger and Oslo. There is no north-south line in western
Norway, however, because of the many fjords.

Airline service is wide-ranging, reaching even the smaller cities.
Scandinavian Airlines (SAS) is jointly owned and operated by three
Scandinavian nations, and the fleet is large and up-to-date.

Tourism is an important source of revenue and jobs. Half a million people from non-Nordic countries visit Norway each year. As
Norway's economy matures and heavy industries decline in importance, tourism and other service industries will be expected to take
up the slack.

Perhaps the most controversial economic question in recent
years has been Norway's relationship to the European Union (EU). In
a 1994 referendum, Norwegians voted against joining the EU, fear-
ing membership would compromise their much-treasured independence. So far, the decision has not adversely affected Norway's economy. Norway remains closely tied with EU nations, which are its
largest trading partners.

Trains that travel from the Bergen railroad station (shown here) to Oslo must pass through more than 200 tunnels. The mountains of Norway have limited the extent of the railroad system.

Social Security, Education, and Health

Norwegians pay about 46 percent of their incomes in taxes. About one-fourth of that goes to their social-welfare system, which is designed to provide security and equal health care and education to all.

In 1967, Norway established the "people's pension." This is paid to retired people, disabled people, and people who cannot otherwise support themselves. The pension ensures that these people have roughly the same standard of living that they would have if they worked, and it is adjusted for inflation and other rises in the cost of living.

The state also pays a family allowance for children under 16 years of age, and employers are required to provide liberal parental leave. Municipal governments provide day-care service for the children of working parents. The idea behind these programs is that raising a family should not cause people any financial hardship.

All citizens are enrolled in a national health-care system that pays for doctors' fees, hospitals, and medicine. There are insurance funds, to which all salaried employees must belong, that provide cash benefits during illness and pregnancy. Self-employed people can participate in these plans if they wish. A public dental service provides dental care to all children. The public health service provides maternal and child care and family counseling to those who need it. Norway has about 1 doctor for every 300 inhabitants, and the infant mortality rate is about 5 per 1,000 live births. Compared to other countries, those are excellent statistics.

Education is free to all, and Norway is working hard to make it universal. Norway's literacy rate is 100 percent, which means that all Norwegians older than 10 years old can read and write. Children are required to attend basic schools, run by the municipalities, from age 6 to age 16. The first five years are primary school; the next three, middle school; and the last three, lower secondary school. Students can go on to upper secondary school if they wish.

Norway has two written languages, Bokmål and Nynorsk. Bokmål (book Norwegian) is based on the dialect that developed in the towns and cities during the long centuries of Danish domination. On the vidda and in the rural valleys, however, different dialects developed. Around the middle of the 19th century, these dialects gave rise to Nynorsk, or "country Norwegian." The dispute over

All Norwegian children between the ages of 6 and 16 must attend basic school. Nearly every Norwegian past the age of 10 can read and write, and Norwegians buy more books per person than readers in any other nation in the world.

which language to use became the focus of a feud between the urban and rural sectors of the population. Finally, Norwegians compromised by making both languages official. Each municipality chooses which to use in its schools. Overall, about 80 percent of the schools use Bokmål.

Fortunately, in speech the dialects are close enough so that any Norwegian, and most Danes and Swedes, can understand both. Likewise, Norwegians understand Danish and Swedish. In addition, from the fifth grade on, every student must take English courses. Elective courses in German and French are popular.

After basic school, most young Norwegians elect to attend upper secondary school for two to three years for vocational training or preparation for college. These schools are also open to adults who want to resume their education. Norway is working hard to expand vocational training in such high-technology fields as computer programming.

After upper secondary school, qualified students can go on to folk high schools, regional colleges, universities, or science colleges.

The folk high school system is attended by about 8,000 students each year. These are boarding schools, first founded more than 100 years ago. The folk schools emphasize the environment, practical skills, and personal growth. There are no tests, and no grades are given. Students, mainly from rural areas, attend for one year.

The regional colleges offer two- to four-year courses for nurses, midwives, physiotherapists, teachers, engineers, and other professionals. Since demand is high, the government expanded the system in 1994, consolidating the 98 regional colleges into 26 state schools.

Norway's university and college system needs expansion, too, even though it has grown by leaps and bounds since World War II. During the centuries of union with Denmark and then with Sweden, people who could afford to do so sent their children to the colleges and universities of the ruling country. The oldest university in the country, Oslo University, is less than 200 years old. But there are full teaching and research universities in Bergen, Trondheim, and Tromsö. In addition, specialized colleges of agriculture, fishing, economics, music, and fine arts attract many students. One college in Oslo even awards graduate and postgraduate degrees in sport and physical education. Still, almost 10 percent of Norway's college students attend schools in other countries.

Norway is rich in colorful Christmas traditions. Both adults and children enjoy feasting, visiting, exchanging presents, and decorating the tree. Young children await the arrival of Father Christmas and the fabled gneiss, *a bearded gnome.*

The People and Culture

Norwegians live in a land that is cold and dark for a good part of the year. The land is rocky, the sea often stormy. It is hard and sometimes dangerous work to wring a living from such an environment. These conditions have produced a hardy, self-reliant people who love the challenges that nature throws at them. They have created wealth out of scarcity and comfort in a harsh landscape.

Many Norwegians work outside, and practically all love to play outside. Nevertheless, they are a very home-loving people. Their homes are tidy, bright, and warm. The windows of most houses or apartments have triple layers of glass to keep out the cold while letting in the light. Lights are abundant; every home has electricity, and it is cheap. Although many new houses have electric heat, quite a few, old and new, are still heated by large painted iron or tile stoves. Bright paintings and handwoven hangings decorate the walls.

It is the dream of every Norwegian to have a holiday cottage as well. Many do, if only by renting one. Some are mountain chalets, modern and roomy. Others are simple huts, with one window and a door. In northern Norway, particularly the Lofoten Islands, *robuer*

Brightly painted Norwegian homes line a lake shore. Many Norwegians also own or rent a vacation cabin on islands off the coasts.

are popular. These are fishermen's shacks, snug wooden cabins on islands and skerries where fishermen took shelter during winter storms. Today they are the home bases for fishing and sailing expeditions or retreats for nature lovers who have spent the week in a crowded city.

Summer's biggest holiday is the Feast of St. John, or Midsummer's Eve, the shortest night of the year. Almost everyone heads for a skerry cottage or a boat with a picnic basket and a blanket. Boats tie up together in inlets and bays. People decorate their boats and cars with birch leaves. Late in the evening, at the first sign of darkness, bonfires break out on every shore. In the cities, there are fireworks along the waterfront, dancing in the streets, and stalls selling sausages and other treats. Everyone stays up to watch the sun rise. The snowy mountaintops turn rosy, then silver, and suddenly the whole scene is bathed with light. Soon everyone is off to bed; the following day, St. John's Day, is a national holiday.

Norwegian rosemaling *(rose painting) is a distinctive folk art practiced by local craftspeople in farm districts. The colorful designs, often based on flowers, decorate walls, ceilings, furniture, and household utensils. The border of this plate can be translated, "The feast is served— Come and get it."*

It sometimes seems that Norwegians are always eating. They normally have four meals a day. Breakfast is cereal, coffee, fish, and bread with jam or cheese. Lunch is usually a short break for one of the tasty open-faced sandwiches, with a cheese or fish spread and elaborate garnishes, called *smörbröd*.

Middag, the Norwegian dinner, takes place at about 4:00 P.M. and consists of huge portions of fish, meat, vegetables, and potatoes. This meal is followed by the afternoon rest, lasting until about 6:30 P.M. It is considered impolite to call on anyone during this time.

Norwegians love to visit and entertain each other, though, later in the evening. They like small groups, and generally prefer to stay at home, perhaps sipping *aquavit* (potato brandy flavored with caraway seeds) or whiskey, telling stories or discussing books. Finally, a late evening supper of sandwiches and tea or coffee closes the day.

People prefer to entertain at home in part because of the strict laws and harsh penalties for drunk driving. Norway has both a conservative Lutheran religious heritage and a long and troubled relationship with alcohol. Drinking, sometimes heavy drinking, is a social problem, especially in the dark and lonely north. Yet spirits have at times been completely illegal, and even today some people disapprove of public drinking.

The official religion of Norway is Evangelical Lutheranism, and about nine-tenths of all citizens are members of the church. The government controls the church, appointing its pastors and officials and paying their salaries. Most Norwegians, however, do not attend services, and the church on the whole is no longer the voice of moral authority for the country.

Norway maintains complete freedom of religion, and there are several active religious organizations, including Baptist, Free Lutheran, Methodist, Catholic, and Christian fundamentalist sects. If Christmas and Easter no longer have the religious significance they once did for most Norwegians, they are still important festivals.

Long before the coming of Christianity, Norway's early inhabitants marked the longest night of the year, December 21, with feasting, sacrifice, and fire, all to ensure the return of the sun. Perhaps these ancient beliefs still color the orgy of feasts and gift giving that is Norway's Christmas.

After weeks of preparing food in advance and buying and wrapping presents, the family puts up the Christmas tree on December 24. They decorate the tree with colored lights and balls and hang paper baskets of nuts and candies on the lower branches. These little treats stay on the tree until January 6, the Feast of the Epiphany.

Nearly everyone attends church on Christmas Eve; afterward people walk home, singing carols, to the major feast. Boiled cod, covered with melted butter, is the main dish. There are also salads, potatoes, roast pork, and cabbage. Dessert is *riskrem* (a rice pudding with fruit sauce) or ice cream. One special treat is *risengrynsgrot*, a pudding of boiled rice and milk served in individual dishes, one of which contains an almond. The person who gets the almond gets an extra gift.

At Easter, instead of staying home or going to church, most Norwegians make one last run to the ski slopes. There they celebrate the end of the long winter by skiing in the spring sunshine, happy in the knowledge that the boating season will soon begin.

There is another side to these hearty, fun-loving outdoorspeople. They are readers, thinkers, and artists. Norwegians buy more books, per person, than the people of any other nation in the world. More than 2,000 new titles are published every year. Norway has produced great playwrights, novelists, musicians, and artists in the past, and the country today is a hotbed of artistic expression.

The most famous Norwegian writer is the dramatist Henrik Ibsen (1828–1906). His realistic plays examined the problems of his society and the inner workings of the human soul. *A Doll's House* (1879) was one of the first and fiercest expressions of the theme of women's repression.

Another writer from Norway's Golden Age, Björnstjerne Björnson (1832–1910), is not so well known outside the country but is loved by Norwegians. He was awarded the Nobel Prize in Literature in 1903, and one of his poems, set to music, has become the national anthem. Its title is *Ja, vi elsker dette landet* (Yes, we love this country).

Other Norwegian Nobel Prize winners include the novelists Knut Hamsun (1859–1952), author of *Mysteries* (1894) and *Growth of the Soil* (1917), and Sigrid Undset, whose novels are still very

Although religion is no longer a major force in most Norwegians' lives, they have carefully preserved their religious heritage. The interior of Fantoft Church shows the detailed wood carving found in stave churches.

Henrik Ibsen's plays have been translated into numerous languages. Some of the plays have been compared to the works of Shakespeare.

popular in Norway. Undset's three-volume historical tale, *Kristin Lavransdatter* (1920–22), is an international classic.

Edvard Munch (1863–1944) is Norway's most widely known painter, chiefly for one often-reproduced painting, *The Scream*. This unforgettable work embodies immense human pain and suffering in a single hollow-eyed figure. Many of Munch's works are emotional and anguished, but he also painted pictures and murals that were full of light and joy. Munch was also a pioneer in graphic arts such as etching, and his work is found today in museums and private collections all over the world.

Norwegians love music, and Norway has produced many world-renowned musicians—composer Edvard Grieg, operatic soprano Kirsten Flagstad, violinist Ole Bull. In 1985, after a guest performance in Paris, critics acclaimed the Norwegian Chamber Orchestra as one of the world's best. The Oslo Symphony Orchestra is respected the world over, and, more important, fills the hall in Oslo. This has not always been true; Norwegians, because of their puritan heritage, do not have a tradition of attending concerts and plays.

Norwegian architecture today is an exciting blend of traditional styles, like that of the stave churches, and modern techniques. Most construction in Norway, including some very large and important buildings, has been in wood, but contemporary architects use steel, glass, and concrete as well as wood to make spacious, exciting, energy-efficient buildings. As befits such a home-loving land, Norwegian architects excel in domestic design.

The Norwegian government is a willing sponsor of all the arts and crafts. The government subsidizes artists and craftspeople with grants, living allowances, and working space. The tradition of the starving artist is dead in Norway.

As with books, more newspapers per person hit the stands and front porches in Norway than in most other industrialized countries. There are over 200 newspapers, and more than 80 of them come out 5 or 6 times a week. (In another instance of the long-lasting puritan influence, Sunday is not a day for newspaper publication.) The daily newspaper circulation is about 66 papers for every 100 people — a remarkably high number.

Newspapers are still the most advanced of the mass media in this land of individualists. But radio and television are catching up. Even though radio and TV reception is hampered by the mountainous landscape of Norway, there is now a radio for every 1.3 people and a television set for every 2.2.

The government held a monopoly on both radio and television transmission for most of the 20th century. Until the government added a second channel in 1981, only one radio channel was broadcast in Norway. Since then, over 400 FM radio stations have cropped up. Though there is still only one nationwide TV network, cable TV, satellite dishes, and commercial advertising have grown increasingly commonplace. And, of course the videocassette player has arrived in Norway.

Nevertheless, television has had a relatively minor effect on the national mind. Norwegians continue to read books and newspapers and to entertain each other with conversation.

The Norwegian film industry has not been, until recently, particularly innovative. The situation is best illustrated by the career of Liv Ullmann, a Norwegian actress of great beauty and acting skill who had to make her career in Swedish films, most notably those of director Ingmar Bergman. No Norwegian director could be so uninhibited and frank about the relationships between men and women as Bergman, because the country was just not ready to accept such explorations on film.

Norwegian filmmakers became more active, daring, and commercially successful in the 1980s. Three important directors were women: Laila Mikkelsen, Anja Breien, and Vibeke Lokkeberg. By the mid-1990s, with help from the Ministry of Cultural Affairs, Norway was producing more films than ever before.

If Norwegians are less daring than the Swedes in exploring inner space, no one has excelled them in the past century in exploring the globe. Maybe it takes desperate weather and hardship to truly bring

Liv Ullmann has appeared in numerous Swedish films, including The Serpent's Egg *and* Autumn Sonata, *both directed by Ingmar Bergman.*

Roald Amundsen was not only the first person to reach the South Pole but also one of the first to fly over the North Pole.

out the Norwegian spirit. Roald Amundsen (1872–1928) was an explorer, a scientist, and an unequaled leader of men. He probed and mapped both the Arctic and the Antarctic reaches. He led the expedition that in 1903 found a sea passage high in the Arctic across North America—the fabled and long-sought Northwest Passage. In 1911, in a stunning dash across a frozen continent, Amundsen and his men beat a British expedition to become the first to reach the South Pole.

Other notable explorers were Thor Heyerdahl (b. 1914) and Fridtjof Nansen (1861–1930). Nansen was more than an explorer and scientist; he was a statesman. In 1922 he won the Nobel Peace Prize for his accomplishments in saving more than 7 million refugees of the Russian revolution from starvation and disease. Heyerdahl's expeditions have taught us about the history of human migration and settlement. Perhaps more important, he has discovered much about the state of the world's oceans and has written passionately about the effect of human garbage and waste on the life of the sea.

Norwegians enjoy a high standard of living, based on a healthy, diversified economy that supports extensive social-welfare programs.

Norway and the Future

Until the 20th century, Norway remained apart from the rest of Europe and the world, protected by the moat of the North Sea. Political domination by Denmark and Sweden delayed the nation's development in many ways, but at the same time it helped to preserve age-old customs and social institutions.

Norway had to grow up fast. Independence and industrialization arrived close together, so that even as the country stepped onto the world stage, it was changing from a stable, if poor, rural society into a world leader in shipping and industry.

Then came the double blows of global depression and war. Norway came face-to-face with the truth that no country can stand alone against poverty or aggression. At the end of World War II, Norwegians faced the double challenge of rebuilding their war-ravaged country and inventing a way for Norway to exist in the modern world.

They met those challenges with the ingenuity and determination developed from centuries of living on Europe's frontier. Norway has become a major industrial nation and a beacon of social justice and security.

New challenges await. As Norway's industrial base gets older, the sources of wealth must change in order to keep the country's standard of living high. All the social programs of which Norwegians are justly proud depend upon a healthy, growing economy.

The economy's health will depend in large part on the oil industry, since revenues from the North Sea and Barents Sea oil fields account for over two-fifths of Norway's export revenues. Also important will be the nation's ability to take full advantage of the hydroelectric power from its rivers and waterfalls. Unlike the energy from oil, coal, and other fossil fuels, hydroelectric power is renewable, as long as rain falls and snow melts in the mountains. This is one natural resource that should continue to prove valuable as time goes by.

Still, if Norway wants to increase its production of metals and continue to grow in other energy-expensive fields, it will have to find other sources of energy. The government has been investigating a number of alternatives. For example, pilot programs for generating energy from wave power have been set up along the rugged coasts.

Another challenge in the future will be environmental protection. Norwegians value their outdoor environment so much, and their lives are so closely entwined with it, that threats to it are seldom taken lightly. In recent decades, acid rain has become one of the greatest threats. All over the industrialized world, the tall smokestacks of power plants and factories send the by-products of burning coal and oil, including sulfuric acid, into the atmosphere. As the wind carries these particles, water condenses around them, and the resulting precipitation is acid rain (or snow), a weak solution of sulfuric acid that can damage various forms of life below.

The lakes, rivers, and forests of Scandinavia in particular have suffered from the effects of acid rain. Miles of forests are full of dead and dying trees, and many lakes and rivers are crystal clear but empty of life.

Norwegian scientists are studying the problem of acid rain, and Norwegian diplomats are working in the United Nations and in the councils of international trade to persuade other nations to control the emissions, or wastes, from their plants and vehicles. For Norway, whose economy and sense of national identity both are dependent on the bounty of nature, the acid rain issue is crucial.

Other forms of pollution threaten Norway directly and indirectly. Oil spills, garbage dumping, and the runoff of pesticides from the rivers of the northern United States, Europe, and Great Britain threaten all life in the North Atlantic. The problem is even worse in the North Sea, because it is a relatively shallow basin with few outlets. And the arctic environment is especially vulnerable, because pollutants last longer in cold, sunless air and water.

Some scientists blame this kind of pollution for sharp reductions since the 1960s in the number of fish available in the ocean and in many rivers and lakes. They also point to catastrophes like

Norwegian scientists are cooperating with researchers from around the world to end the spread of such sights as this—trees killed by acid rain.

the mass death of North Sea seals in the late 1980s as proof that humanity's ability to foul its nest is outstripping nature's capacity for self-renewal. Because their very way of life is at stake, Norwegians follow such issues with greater passion than most.

While Norway must work to remain a leader in the world economy, the country must deal with the social consequences of its success. Rapid change, many Norwegians feel, has weakened the social fabric. The shift of population from country to city has broken family ties. The state religion has lost much of its moral authority, and no other institution has replaced it. The divorce rate has risen, as have crime rates and problems with drugs.

These difficulties are less pressing in Norway than in many other industrialized nations. Most Norwegians are stable, healthy people. Family values are strong. Norwegians have a habit of mind that is inward looking and somewhat self-critical; just as they are quick to see problems in their society, however, so are they quick to look for solutions.

The brightest hopes for Norway's future rest with its children. Thanks to the nation's program of social services they are healthier, stronger, and better educated than ever before. And they will face the challenges of the future with the same Norwegian blend of canny determination and self-reliance that has brought Norway this far.

◄ G L O S S A R Y ►

acid rain
: Precipitation polluted with sulfuric acid, a by-product of the burning of fossil fuels. Acid rain is said by some scientists to be responsible for the death of forests and freshwater life.

amber
: Fossilized tree resin; a hard, translucent yellow-brown substance that was used in jewelry and ornaments in ancient times.

aquavit
: Potato brandy flavored with caraway seeds.

Arctic Circle
: The imaginary circle around the earth at about 66° north of the equator; the lower limit of the northern frigid zone.

Bronze Age
: The period in human civilization marked by the ability to make tools and weapons out of bronze, an alloy of copper and tin. In Norway, the Bronze Age began about 2000 B.C.

capitalism
: The economic and political theory that society functions best when private ownership of property and the profit motive are the incentives for individuals to produce goods and services. See socialism.

Gulf Stream
: A warm current in the North Atlantic Ocean flowing from the Gulf of Mexico northeast along the coast of the United States to Nantucket, then across the ocean past the British Isles to the North Sea.

Hanseatic League
: A 12th- to 15th-century association of independent cities within the Germanic area of the Holy Roman Empire.

Iron Age The period of civilization marked by the smelting of iron and its use in tools and weapons. Preceded by the Bronze and Stone ages, the Iron Age began around 1500 B.C. in western Asia, somewhat later in northern Europe.

maelstrom A powerful, often violent whirlpool that sucks in objects within a certain radius; this word from Old Norse also means anything, such as a storm or an argument, that resembles a whirlpool in turbulence.

marten A slender, fur-bearing, carnivorous mammal, related to but larger than the weasel.

referendum The act of submitting a policy question to the direct vote of the people.

runes Characters of the alphabet developed from Latin and Greek letters by the German and Scandinavian tribes from the 3rd to 13th centuries.

sable A carnivorous mammal of northern Europe and Asia, related to the marten; its dark brown fur is highly prized.

Scandinavia The region centered around the Baltic Sea, consisting of Sweden, Norway, Denmark, Finland, and Iceland.

socialism The economic and political theory that society functions best when the government or the people as a group own and control property and the means of producing goods and distributing goods. See capitalism.

steppe A dry, treeless plain of wind-deposited soil covered with grasses and other plants that tolerate arid conditions.

vidda High mountain plateaus or plains.

‹ I N D E X ›